ROY CAMPBELL

Selected Poems

ROY CAMPBELL

Selected Poems

Edited and introduced
by Joseph Pearce

Chavagnes Studium Press

MMXVIII

CHAVAGNES

Chavagnes Studium Press
www.chavagnes.org/press

Text of the poetry is now in the public domain.
Design, selection and introduction © Chavagnes Studium Press, 2018.

First published by Saint Austin Press, London, 2001.

This book is sold subject to the condition that it shall not, by way of trade or otherwise, be lent, re-sold, hired out or otherwise circulated without the publisher's prior consent in any form of binding or cover other than that in which it is published and without a similar condition including this condition being imposed on the subsequent purchaser. All rights reserved. No part of this publication may be reproduced or transmitted in any form or by any means, electronic or mechanical including photocopying, recording or any information storage or retrieval system, without prior permission in writing from the publishers.

For Susannah

But when the Muse or some as lovely sprite,
Friend, lover, wife, in such a form as thine,
Thrilling a mortal frame with half her light
And choosing for her guise such eyes and hair
  As scarcely veil the subterfuge divine,
Descends with him his lonely fight to share ...

CONTENTS

Introduction ... xv

Dedication to Mary Campbell ... 1

The Theology of Bongwi, the Baboon ... 3

From *The Flaming Terrapin* ... 3

The Serf ... 5

Zulu Song ... 6

The Zulu Girl ... 6

To a Pet Cobra ... 7

The Zebras ... 9

The Sisters ... 9

On Some South African Novelists ... 10

On the Same ... 10

On Professor Drennan's Verse ... 11

Georgian Spring ... 11

From *The Georgiad* ... 12

Mazeppa ... 19

Saint Peter of the Three Canals ... 23

The Albatross ... 27

Tristan da Cunha ... 32

Horses on the Camargue ... 36

Mass at Dawn ... 37

Autumn ... 38

Choosing a Mast ... 38

Posada ... 41

Driving Cattle to Casas Buenas ... 41

From *Mithraic Emblems*:
The Seven Swords ... 42
The Morning ... 43
San Juan Sings ... 44
Mithras Speaks 1 ... 44
Mithras Speaks 2 ... 45

To the Sun ... 46

The Fight ... 46

To "the Future" ... 48

Toledo, July 1936 ... 48

Hot Rifles ... 49

Christ in Uniform ... 50

The Alcazar Mined ... 50

To My Jockey ... 51

The Carmelites of Toledo ... 52

La Mancha in Wartime ... 60

To Mary after the Red Terror ... 61

SELECTED POEMS

"Poems for Spain" ... 62

From *Flowering Rifle* ... 63

From "A Letter from the San Mateo Front" ... 68

The Prodigal ... 69

The Hoopoe ... 70

The Clock in Spain ... 75

One Transport Lost ... 81

Luis de Camoes ... 83

Imitation (and Endorsement) of the Famous Sonnet of Bocage Which He Wrote on Active Service Out East ... 84

Dreaming Spires ... 84

The Skull in the Desert ... 89

The Beveridge Plan ... 93

Monologue ... 93

Auguries ... 97

Reflections ... 99

Washing Day ... 101

Rhapsody of the Man in Hospital Blues and the "Hyde Park Lancers" ... 102

Arion ... 105

Ska-hawtch Wha Hae! ... 106

The Drummer Boy's Catechism (An Essay in Hopkinese) ... 109

Inscape of Skytehawks on the Cookhouse Roof (In Homage to Gerard Manley Hopkins) ... 111

San Juan de la Cruz ... 113

Upon a gloomy night (trans from St John of the Cross) ... 114

Verses Written after an Ecstasy of High Exaltation (trans from St John of the Cross) ... 115

The Soul which Suffers with Impatience to See God (trans from St John of the Cross) ... 117

Concerning Christ and the Soul (trans from St John of the Cross)... 119

Song of the Soul that is glad to know God by Faith (trans from St John of the Cross) ... 120

Of the communion of the three Persons (trans from St John of the Cross) ... 122

On Lisi's Golden Hair (trans from Quevedo) ... 123

Counsel (trans from Bandeira) ... 124

The Shadow of My Soul (trans from Lorca) ... 124

Rain (trans from Lorca) ... 126

The Song of the Honey (trans from Lorca) ... 127

Elegy (trans from Lorca) ... 129

Merry-go-round (trans from Lorca) ... 132

They Cut Down Three Trees (trans from Lorca) ... 133

SELECTED POEMS

Benediction (trans from Baudelaire) ... 134

I love the thought of those old naked days (trans from Baudelaire) ... 137

The Carcase (trans from Baudelaire) ... 138

The Duel (trans from Baudelaire) ... 140

Drunken Boat (trans from Rimbaud) ... 141

The thing that hurts and wrings (trans from Pessoa) ... 145

Death comes before its time (trans from Pessoa) ... 145

The poet fancying each belief (trans from Pessoa) ... 146

From *The Maritime Ode* (trans from Campos/Pessoa) ... 147

After Rubén Darío ... 148

Nativity ... 149

Autobiography in Fifty Kicks ... 150

¡Caramba! ... 153

Twin Reflections ... 153

November Nights ... 155

From "Fragments from 'The Golden Shower'" ... 156

INTRODUCTION

Roy Campbell was, in the judgement of T. S. Eliot and Edith Sitwell, one of the finest poets of his generation. From the publication of *The Flaming Terrapin* in 1924 to the appearance of his masterly translation of the poems of St John of the Cross a quarter of a century later, he exhibited a prodigious if sometimes prodigal talent.

According to a reviewer in the *Spectator*, *The Flaming Terrapin* was "like a breath of new youth, like a love-affair to a lady in her fifties." "We wanted air," wrote a reviewer in the *New Statesman*, "and here is a south-wester straight from the sea." It was also, to many reviewers, a breath of fresh air that blew away both the banal rustications of the Georgians and the stale nihilism of the new generation of pseudo-sceptics.

> ... in this extraordinary poem we are far from the mimble-mamble of the slim-volumed Georgians, as far too from the elegant nervosities of pseudo-Eliots and pseudo-Cocteaus. Full circle! We have spun back ... back to an exuberant relish of the sheer sonority and clangour of words, words enjoyed for their own gust, and flung down to fit each other with an easy rapture of phrase.

In similar vein, George Russell in the *Irish Statesman* hailed Campbell as a newly emergent giant of literature.

> Among a crowd of poets writing delicate verses he moves like a mastodon with shaggy sides pushing through a herd of lightfoot antelopes ... No poet I have read for many years excites me to more speculation about his future, for I do not know of any new poet who has such a savage splendour of epithet or who can marry the wild word so fittingly to the wild thought.

Ironically perhaps, the exciting new poet owed more to the dynamic tradition of the Elizabethans than to the innovative inanities of many of his contemporaries. Paradoxically, the blast of fresh air was also a blast from the past. "By Jove they are marvellous poets," he would write in 1926, remarking of Thomas Dekker's *The Pleasant Comedy of Old Fortunatus* that it was "full of enough poetry to set up half a dozen modern poets". The Elizabethans were full of a "bombast and fire" that inflamed Campbell's creativity.

> I am absolutely drunk with these fellows. They wrote poetry just as a machine-gun fires off bullets. They couldn't stop writing it. They don't even stop to get their breath. They go thundering on until you forget everything about the sense and ... end up in a positive debauch of thunder and splendour and music. Everything that disparaging critics say about the Elizabethans may be true. They are raw, careless, headstrong, coarse, brutal. But how vivid they are, how intoxicated with their own imagination ... For three years I have been reading the Russians hard and the modern French but this is like having a wild Saturday night after a week of Sundays.

In this intoxicated and intoxicating letter, Campbell was giving a tantalising glimpse of the underlying influences animating his own verse. The flamboyance of the Elizabethans had coloured the imagery in *The Flaming Terrapin* with a vivid sharpness distinguishing it from most other contemporary verse in much the same way that the vivid sharpness of the Pre-Raphaelites had stood out from the monochrome subtleties of impressionism. He was also prophesying the spirit of his future satires. In describing the "bombast and fire", the writing of poetry "just as a machine-gun fires off bullets", the failure to stop to catch one's breath, the "thundering on until you forget everything about the sense and end up in a positive debauch of thunder and splendour and music," Campbell is describing his own satires, still to be written. *The Wayzgoose*, *The Georgiad*, *Flowering Rifle* and *Talking Bronco* would be "raw, careless, headstrong, coarse, brutal" and would be written in a breathless stream of invective, in stark contrast to the care he took with his lyric verse.

Following his brazenly blazing debut with *The Flaming Terrapin*, Campbell's subsequent poetic output can be compartmentalised chronologically as follows: the African poems, mostly written after the poet's return to his native South Africa in 1924; the Bloomsbury poems, written in response to his experiences with, and his reactions to, the Bloomsbury group in 1927 and 1928; the Provencal poems, inspired by the poet's life in Provence following his "escape" from Bloomsbury; the Spanish poems, offering a potent evocation of the poet's impressions of the Spanish civil war; the later poems, embracing the poet's war-time experiences, his post-war political scepticism and his subsequent mellowing; and, finally, his verse translations.

Though most of Campbell's African poems were not written until his return to South Africa in the mid-twenties, "The Theology of Bongwi, the Baboon" is from an earlier period, dating either from before he left South Africa or from shortly after his arrival in Oxford early in 1919. It expresses a youthful religious scepticism, indicating that the teenage poet had moved away from a lukewarm and half-hearted acceptance of his parents' Presbyterianism towards an inarticulate agnosticism. "The Theology of Bongwi, the Baboon" is an amusingly irreverent verse possibly inspired by Yeats's poem "An Indian Upon God" in which a meditative Indian hears a moorfowl declaring that God is "an undying moorfowl", and a lotus proclaiming that "He hangeth upon a stalk". Yet Campbell's verse, for all its playful theological subversion, is devoid of the cynical world-weariness which is the mark of so much iconoclastic anti-religious satire. Instead, it is filled with a mischievous rumbustiousness, a spiritual *joie de vivre*, which has more in common with the playful satirical verse of G.K. Chesterton. If "The Theology of Bongwi, the Baboon" is compared with "Race Memory (by a dazed Darwinian)", a satirical poem on a similar theme by Chesterton, the deep-rooted affinity is instantly apparent.

An altogether darker theme pervades many of the other African poems. In "The Serf", "Zulu Song" and "The Zulu Girl", the underlying tension between the races is combined with a deep-rooted sympathy for the plight and the resentment of the Zulu people.

> Yet in that drowsy stream his flesh imbibes
> An old unquenched unsmotherable heat -
> The curbed ferocity of beaten tribes,
> The sullen dignity of their defeat.

The smouldering and unsmotherable resentment, the curbed ferocity looming like a harbinger of doom ... In the light of future events in Campbell's native country, his words convey more than a hint of prophecy.

"The Zebras", another of the African poems, is not merely an early indication of Campbell's prowess as a nature poet, but is an affirmation that his vision of nature clashes dramatically with that of his contemporaries. Campbell disliked the saccharine sweetness of the Georgians, satirising in "Georgian Spring" their sterile depictions of torpid and tepid rural life. In contrast, his own vision of nature was as wild and untamed as the continent that gave it birth. "The Zebras", in common with later poems such as "Horses on the Camargue", pulsates with hot-blooded instinct, untroubled and untrammelled by the constraints of anthropocentric convention. It is not the poetry of nature domesticated but of nature rampant. Similarly, the early eroticism of "The Sisters", untroubled and untrammelled by the inherent hypocrisy of puritanism, foreshadows the potent combination of carnality and spirituality which would be consummated in Campbell's love poems to his wife.

Paradoxically, the life-assertiveness and sexuality of the African poems was linked to Campbell's antagonism towards the Freudian gospel of self-gratification and, more specifically, to his rejection of the sexual *mores* of the Bloomsbury group.

Campbell believed that sex was not a subject for morbid fascination but was a glorious mystery to be enjoyed in the purity of passion. When attempts are made to strip it of its mystery it is simultaneously stripped of its higher meaning. All that remains when sex is removed from the glory of its romantic heights is a gaudy remnant festering in the furtive frustrations of its sterile depths. Sex, as preached and practised in Bloomsbury, was the omnipotence of impotence. This is the *leit-motif* which predominates in *The Georgiad*, Campbell's satire of the Bloomsburys. Androgyno, the poem's hero, is so shocking to the puritanically prurient sensibilities of Bloomsbury because he flouts their adolescent furtiveness in an unrestrained fertility rite. Androgyno is the shamelessly potent vanquisher of psycho-sexual impotence, the exorciser of Bloomsbury's perverse spirit.

In subjecting sex to the presuppositions of psychology or psycho-analysis, Campbell believed that self-appointed "experts" were stripping it of its joy, its beauty, its meaning - and ultimately even the pleasure it had to offer.

> He roars with agony at Venus' thrill
> And takes his pleasures as a bitter pill
> Or social duty, much against his will;
> And when he leaps enthroned in stallion state,
> Less with hot flame, than pedantry, elate,
> Ponders the physiology of birth,
> And strives, of sex, "the meaning" to unearth:
> And, if he found it, would not stop to breathe
> But straight the sex of meaning would unsheathe,
> And, even that discovered, would not wait,
> But work out its relation to "the State" ...

Related to Campbell's rejection of the fundamental tenets of Freudianism is his rejection of those who seek to make "happiness" a servile subject of psychology or the intellect. In *The Georgiad* he snorts contempt at those who studied Bertrand Russell's "melancholy recipes for 'happiness'."

> All who in Russell's burly frame admire
> The "lineaments of gratified desire" ...
> All who of "Happiness" have learned the ropes
> From Bertrand Russell or from Marie Stopes.

As with so much of Campbell's satire, *The Georgiad*'s invective is too vindictive. It is all too often spoilt by spite. This underlying weakness has obscured the more serious points its author sought to make. Embedded between the attacks on Bertrand Russell, Marie Stopes, Vita Sackville-West, Virginia Woolf and a host of other Bloomsburys and Georgians are classically refined objections to the prevailing philosophy of scepticism, mounted like pearls of wisdom in the basest of metal. "Nor knew the Greeks, save in the laughing page, The philosophic emblem of our age" ... The "damp philosophy" of the modern world, as espoused by the archetypal modern poet, was responsible for the prevailing pessimism and disillusionment of the post-war world. In preaching such a philosophy, which was "the fountain-source of all his woes", the poet's "damp philosophy" left him "damp in spirit". Nihilism was self-negating. It was the philosophy of the self-inflicted wound.

In the rejection of post-war pessimism and its nihilistic ramifications - a rejection which had been as implicit in *The Flaming Terrapin* as it had been explicit in *The Georgiad* - Campbell was uniting himself spiritually with others, such as T.S. Eliot and Evelyn Waugh, who were similarly seeking glimmers of philosophical light amidst the prevailing gloom. In his case, as in theirs, the philosophical search would lead to orthodox Christianity.

In his early verse, and particularly in *The Flaming Terrapin*, a confused Christianity is infused into the confusion of influences that had dominated at Oxford. Reality, in its artistic, political, philosophical and theological manifestations, is seen through the poetic prism of Nietzsche, Darwin and Einstein. There is an idolisation of the Nietzschean "strong" and an idealisation of the Darwinian "fittest". There is a hope that those who were "ennobled" by the sufferings of the war will triumph over demoralisation and despair. Beneath the surface, submerged but omnipotent like the Terrapin itself, is the hidden influence of Eliot's *The Waste Land* with its post-war angst and superficial cynicism pointing towards possible resurrection.

For Campbell, the forces of resurrection, in the form of creation, or re-creation, are symbolised in *The Flaming Terrapin* by the Terrapin itself.

> The Flaming Terrapin that towed the Ark
> Rears up his hump of thunder on the dark,
> And like a mountain, seamed with rocky scars,
> Tufted with forests, barnacled with stars,
> Crinkles with rings, as from its ancient sleep,
> Into a foam of life he wakes the Deep.

The Flaming Terrapin is a neo-pagan hymn to Life transfused with mystic symbolism. The Rainbow, the symbol of the fruitful union of the Earth and the Sun, is a "blaze of watery fire". The feminine Earth feels the Sun's "fiery manhood swim" through trembling earth and limb,

> Huge spasms rend her, as in red desire
> He leaps and fills her gushing womb with fire ...

At its deepest, *The Flaming Terrapin* conveys a promise, at this stage both inarticulate and unfulfilled, of the poet's emerging mysticism and spirituality. It offers a premonition of the poet's own future, a prophecy of a paganism christened, fertilised by faith and reborn. In the early part of the poem there is a profound insight into the spiritual basis of all matter which is reminiscent of Christian philosophers such as Duns Scotus and Christian poets such as Gerard Manley Hopkins and G.K. Chesterton. In spite of Campbell's later satirical lampoons of Hopkins, there is more than a trace of the Jesuit poet's concept of *inscape* in the following passage from *The Flaming Terrapin*,

> Action and flesh cohere in one clean fusion
> Of force with form: the very ethers breed
> Wild harmonies of song: the frailest reed
> Holds shackled thunder in its heart's seclusion.
> And every stone that lines my lonely way,
> Sad tongueless nightingale without a wing,
> Seems on the point of rising up to sing
> And donning scarlet for its dusty grey!

Although *The Flaming Terrapin* had signified an embryonic mysticism, and *The Georgiad* a mind at war with intellectual modernism, their author still had no ordered or coherent philosophy with which to develop the one or strengthen the other. Having diagnosed the folly of materialism and the disease of modernity he was uncertain of the cure and was left groping with little more than fragments or figments of a truth only dimly perceived. This groping after truth found expression in the sequence of sonnets, *Mithraic Emblems*, which collectively are the most obscure and oblique of all his verse.

Campbell had become interested in Mithraism in Provence where the earliest of the sonnets were written. Relics of Mithraism, which struggled with Christianity for the hearts and minds of Europeans during the declining centuries of the Roman Empire, are scattered throughout Provence where Christian churches are often built on the site of previous Mithraic shrines. In many respects, Mithraism, which rated strength and nobility over meekness and humility, was seen as the religion of the soldier whereas Christianity was the religion of the slave. For Campbell, with his love for classical antiquity and for the martial spirit of Rome Triumphant, Mithraism seemed a more natural home than Christianity. Interwoven with his preference for the faith of the warrior was his attraction to the mystical myth, rooted in tauromachy, at the heart of Mithraism. The forces of life in Mithraism are symbolised by a wild bull, the sacrifice of which by Mithras brought forth all the fruits of the earth. Thus, in Campbell's fertile imagination, the courage of the arena took on a mystical transcendence, a ritualistic re-enactment of the sacrificial miracle of Life. The bullfight was more than a mere sport, it was a spiritual sacrifice.

This potent imagery, reinforced by the Mithraic worship of the light-giving and life-giving power of the Sun, combined to form and frame the inspiration for, and the aspirations of, the sonnets. The sense of obscurity is heightened by the overlaying of other Mithraic emblems on to the fundamental fabric and design, such as the image of the raven as a messenger of the Sun-God, or of the snake and the scorpion as images of the hateful designs of the Evil One. Yet this array of mythical images was not enough to satisfy Campbell's mystical quest. He christens his Mithraism by the addition of specifically Catholic imagery, such as the seven sorrowful swords that pierced the heart of the Blessed Virgin following the Passion of her Son.

Taken as a whole, *Mithraic Emblems* displays a soul in transit. The earliest sonnets, written in Provence, show the poet groping with an uncomprehended and incomprehensible paganism, relishing the irrational, the *obscurum per obscurius* - the obscure by the still more obscure. It is Mithraic "truth" whispered with masonic secrecy - the affirmation of faith without reason. In the later sonnets, written in Spain, Christianity emerges triumphant, not so much to vanquish Mithraism as to make sense of it. The towering influence of St John of the Cross, the great Spanish poet and mystic, emerges as a herald of divine revelation, a surrogate St John the Baptist preparing the way for the Coming of Christ. At the end of the sequence Mithras himself speaks, confessing that he, the god identified with the sun, is but a servant of the one True God.

> ... "We work for the same Boss
> though you are earth and I a star,
> and herdsmen both, though my guitar
> is strung to strum the world across!

He, Mithras, serves the same God as does the poet, the God who won His victory on the Cross ...

> under the stretched, terrific wings,
> the outspread arms (our soaring King's) -
> the man they made an Albatross!

The final sonnet, addressed "To The Sun", is the poet's unequivocal affirmation of Christian faith.

> Oh let your shining orb grow dim,
> Of Christ the mirror and the shield,
> That I may gaze through you to Him,
> See half the miracle revealed ...

The twenty-three sonnets which comprise the *Mithraic Emblems* represent the story of a soul's conversion. Beginning with the seeds of Mithraic uncertainty, planted in Provence, the soul's transformation would finally bear fruit in the fertile and faithful soil of Spain, described by Campbell "as a country to which I owe everything as having saved my soul".

Roy and Mary Campbell were received into the Catholic Church in June 1935. A year later the priest who received them was murdered by communist militiamen at the outbreak of Spain's fratricidal civil war. The Campbells would lose other friends during the war, including the martyred Carmelites of Toledo whom they had befriended and sheltered. Campbell's conversion, and the bloody conflict that followed in its wake, inspired some of his finest verse, including "The Fight",

"Toledo, July 1936", "The Alcazar Mined", "La Mancha in Wartime" and "To Mary after the Red Terror".

Campbell's siding with Catholic Spain against the forces of the communist Republic during the civil war ensured his alienation from the socialist and secular intelligentsia and literati. For much of the remainder of his life he was embroiled in bitter disputes with an ever expanding array of enemies. His attacks on the left-wing poets of the thirties, such as Spender, Auden, Day-Lewis, MacNeice and MacDiarmid, confirmed his marginalisation in an increasingly liberal and secular world. For many of the rising generation of poets and critics Campbell was anathema, a literary untouchable. He became a martyr to "political correctness" long before the term was invented.

In spite of such adversity, or perhaps because of it, he continued to write verse of considerable merit, both during and after the second world war. Brilliant post-war parodies of Hugh MacDiarmid ("Ska-hawtch Wha Hae!") and Gerard Manley Hopkins ("The Drummer Boy's Catechism" and "Inscape of Skytehawks on the Cookhouse Roof") displayed a rumbustious wit so often smothered in his earlier satires by excessive spitefulness. His acclaimed and ever popular translations of the poems of St John of the Cross did much to restore his tarnished reputation, and late poems such as "Nativity" proved that he had not lost the power to write religious verse of great sensitivity, insight and beauty.

Campbell was killed in a car crash on his way back from the Holy Week celebrations in Seville on 23 April 1957 and it is tempting to see a symbolic symmetry in the violent nature of his death. Ever a man of action, real and imagined, he had endured, and even occasionally enjoyed, the violent aspects of life. He died, it seems, as he had lived. Not for him the slow subsidence into sickness and a protracted, deathbed-bound exit. The self-styled soldier poet had died with his boots on. The symbolism was not lost on Edith Sitwell who heard of Campbell's death during a visit to New York:

This simple giant, with "devocioun in his heart", was the true Knight of Our Lady, and if he had to be taken by death, it was suitable that this should have been when he was returning from the celebration of Her Son's Resurrection. I think, too, that he, who was all energy, all fire, would have hated to die slowly and helplessly, in bed. He died, as he had lived, like a flash of lightning.

One wonders whether Sitwell had also noticed that her champion, the knight who had defended her own reputation against the attacks of various literary dragons, had been killed on the feast of St George.

The final word should be left to the poet himself:

> For only out of solitude or strife
> Are born the sons of valour and delight;
> And lastly for her rich, exulting life,
> That with the wind stopped not its singing breath
> But carolled on, the louder for its death.

Dedication to Mary Campbell[1]

When in dead lands where men like brutish herds
Rush to and fro by aimless frenzies borne,
Firing a golden fusillade of words,
Lashing his laughter like a knotted scourge,
A poet of his own disdain is born
And dares among the rabble to emerge –

His humble townsfolk sicken to behold
This monstrous changeling whom they schooled in vain,
Who brings no increase to their hoard of gold,
Who lives by sterner laws than they have known
And worships, even where their idols reign,
A god superbly stronger than their own.

Accursèd in the temples of the Pagan
His evil fame is borne on every wind:
His name is thundered by the priests of Dagon[2]
And all Philistia whispers with the plot
To shear his sleeping head, his eyes to blind,
And chain his ankle to a trundling shot;

For That which o'er their cities far-espied
Decreed his spirit like a torch to shine
Has fired him with the peacock's flaunting pride
Who still would fan his embers to a blaze
Though it were but to startle grunting swine
Or herds of sleepy cattle to amaze.

Insulting their dull sense with gorgeous dyes,
The matador of truth, he trails his scorn
Before their lowered horns and bloodshot eyes –

---

[1] This was the dedicatory verse to Campbell's first edition of *Collected Poems*.
[2] Philistine idol.

For never can their stubborn necks be tamed
Until they know how laughter must be borne
And learn to look on beauty unashamed.

Even this were victory, though by his foes
On every side with plunging hoofs beset,
Reeling at last beneath their leaden blows,
Behind some heap of filth he should be flung
Whereon the spider spreads his dusty net
And the cold viper hatches out her young.
But when the Muse or some as lovely sprite,
Friend, lover, wife, in such a form as thine,
Thrilling a mortal frame with half her light
And choosing for her guise such eyes and hair
As scarcely veil the subterfuge divine,
Descends with him his lonely fight to share –

He knows his gods have watched him from afar,
And he may take her beauty for a sign
That victory attends him as a star,
Shaped like a Valkyrie for his delight
In lovely changes through the day to shine
And be the glory of the long blue night.

When my spent heart had drummed its own retreat,
You rallied the red squadron of my dreams,
Turning the crimson rout of their defeat
Into a white assault of seraphim
Invincibly arrayed with flashing beams
Against a night of spectres foul and grim.

Sweet sister; through all earthly treasons true,
My life has been the enemy of slumber:
Bleak are the waves that lash it, but for you
And your clear faith, I am a locked lagoon
That circles with its jagged reef of thunder
The calm blue mirror of the stars and moon.

The Theology of Bongwi, the Baboon

This is the wisdom of the Ape
    Who yelps beneath the Moon –
'Tis God who made me in His shape
    He is a Great Baboon.
'Tis He who tilts the moon askew
    And fans the forest trees,
The heavens which are broad and blue
    Provide him his trapeze;
He swings with tail divinely bent
    Around those azure bars
And munches to his Soul's content
    The kernels of the stars;
And when I die, His loving care
    Will raise me from the sod
To learn the perfect Mischief there,
    The Nimbleness of God.

From *The Flaming Terrapin*

Towering like a steeple through the air
He stalks: the cascades of his molten hair
With streams of lava wash his ebon limbs:
His eyes, like wheels of fire with whirling rims,
Revolve in his gaunt skull, from which a tusk
Curves round his ear and glitters in the dusk.
Now he comes prowling on the ravaged earth,
He whores with Nature, and she brings to birth
Monsters perverse, and fosters feeble minds,
Nourishing them on stenches such as winds
Lift up from rotting whales. On earth again
Foul Mediocrity begins his reign:
All day, all night God stares across the curled

Rim of the vast abyss upon the world:
All night, all day the world with eyes as dim
Gazes as fatuously back at him.
He does not hear the forests when they roar
Some second purging deluge to implore,
When cities from his ancient rule revolt,
He grasps, but dares not wield, his thunderbolt.
Sodom, rebuilded, scorns the wilting power
That once played skittles with her tallest tower.
Each Nation's banner, like a stinking clout,
Infecting Earth's four winds, flaunts redly out,
Dyed with the bloody issues of a war,
For hordes of cheering victims to adore.
While old Plutocracy on gouty feet
Limps like a great splay camel down the street;
And Patriotism, Satan's angry son,
Rasps on the trigger of his rusty gun,
While priests and churchmen, heedless of the strife,
Find remedy in thoughts of afterlife;
Had they nine lives, O muddled and perplexed,
They'd waste each one in thinking of the next!
Contentment, like an eating slow disease,
Settles upon them, fetters hands and knees;
While pale Corruption, round his ghastly form
Folding the cloudy terrors of the storm,
His shapeless spectre smothered in the blending
Of heavy fumes, o'er mirky towns descending,
Swims through the reek, with movements as of one
Who, diving after pearls, down from the sun
Along the shaft of his own shadow slides
With knife in grinning jaws; and as he glides,
Nearing the twilight of the nether sands,
Under him swings his body deft and slow,
Gathers his knees up, reaches down his hands
And settles on his shadow like a crow.
So dread Corruption, over human shoals,
Instead of pearls, comes groping after souls,

And the pure pearl of many a noble life
Falls to the scraping of his rusty knife.
Till glutted with his spoil, like some huge squid,
He reascends, in smeary vapours hid,
And, like those awful nightmares of the deep
When through the gloom propelled with backward sweep
Out of their mirky bowels they discharge
The dark hydraulic jet that moves their large
Unwieldy trunks – back to his secret lair
He welters through the dense miasmal air
In inky vapours cloaking his retreat:
Ever-renewed, his soft and sucking feet
Break from his trunk, and wandering alone,
Grow into forms as ghastly as his own:
Which, in their turn, with equal vigour breed
And through the world disseminate his seed,
Till over every city, grim and vast,
The shadow of a brooding death is cast.

The Serf

His naked skin clothed in the torrid mist
That puffs in smoke around the patient hooves,
The ploughman drives, a slow somnambulist,
And through the green his crimson furrow grooves.
His heart, more deeply than he wounds the plain,
Long by the rasping share of insult torn,
Red clod, to which the war-cry once was rain
And tribal spears the fatal sheaves of corn,
Lies fallow now. But as the turf divides
I see in the slow progress of his strides
Over the toppled clods and falling flowers,
The timeless, surly patience of the serf
That moves the nearest to the naked earth
And ploughs down palaces, and thrones, and towers.

Zulu Song[3]

Great must be this people that,
    one strong purpose binding,
Is like a great black snake along
    the valleys winding,
Whose scales are shields, whose
    teeth are spears, who thunders
    as he goes,
Whose crests of feathers flutter
    like the faint hearts of his foes,
Who rises in the daybreak from
    the forest dark and cool,
And goes to drink at sunset from
    the crimson coloured pool.

The Zulu Girl

When in the sun the hot red acres smoulder,
Down where the sweating gang its labour plies,
A girl flings down her hoe, and from her shoulder
Unslings her child tormented by the flies.

She takes him to a ring of shadow pooled
By thorn-trees: purpled with the blood of ticks,
While her sharp nails, in slow caresses ruled,
Prowl through his hair with sharp electric clicks,

---

[3] Published in an article entitled "Roy Campbell: A Fighting Catholic Poet Remembered", by Neville Braybrooke in *The Southern Cross*, 16 May 1982. Braybrooke commented: "During the 1940's Campbell gave me a translation of a Zulu war song...for my quarterly *The Wind and the Rain*. He spoke Zulu fluently..."

His sleepy mouth, plugged by the heavy nipple,
Tugs like a puppy, grunting as he feeds:
Through his frail nerves her own deep languors ripple
Like a broad river sighing through its reeds.

Yet in that drowsy stream his flesh imbibes
An old unquenched unsmotherable heat –
The curbed ferocity of beaten tribes,
The sullen dignity of their defeat.

Her body looms above him like a hill
Within whose shade a village lies at rest,
Or the first cloud so terrible and still
That bears the coming harvest in its breast.

To a Pet Cobra

With breath indrawn and every nerve alert,
As at the brink of some profound abyss,
I love on my bare arm, capricious flirt,
To feel the chilly and incisive kiss
Of your lithe tongue that forks its swift caress
Between the folded slumber of your fangs,
And half reveals the nacreous recess
Where death upon those dainty hinges hangs.

Our lonely lives in every chance agreeing,
It is no common friendship that you bring,
It was the desert starved us into being,
The hate of men that sharpened us to sting:
Sired by starvation, suckled by neglect,
Hate was the surly tutor of our youth:
I too can hiss the hair of men erect
Because my lips are venomous with truth.

Where the hard rock is barren, scorched the spring,
Shrivelled the grass, and the hot wind of death
Hornets the crag with whirred metallic wing –
We drew the fatal secret of our breath:
By whirlwinds bugled forth, whose funnelled suction
Scrolls the spun sand into a golden spire,
Our spirits leaped, hosannas of destruction,
Like desert lilies forked with tongues of fire.

Dainty one, deadly one, whose folds are panthered
With stars, my slender Kalahari flower,
Whose lips with fangs are delicately anthered,
Whose coils are volted with electric power,
I love to think how men of my dull nation
Might spurn your sleep with inadvertent heel
To kindle up the lithe retaliation
And caper to the slash of sudden steel.

There is no sea so wide, no waste so steril
But holds a rapture for the sons of strife:
There shines upon the topmost peak of peril
A throne for spirits that abound in life:
There is no joy like theirs who fight alone,
Whom lust or gluttony have never tied,
Who in their purity have built a throne,
And in their solitude a tower of pride.

I wish my life, O suave and silent sphinx,
Might flow like yours in some such strenuous line,
My days the scales, my years the bony links,
The chain the length of its resilient spine:
And when at last the moment comes to strike,
Such venom give my hilted fangs the power,
Like drilling roots the dirty soil that spike,
To sting these rotted wastes into a flower.

The Zebras

From the dark woods that breathe of fallen showers,
Harnessed with level rays in golden reins,
The zebras draw the dawn across the plains
Wading knee-deep among the scarlet flowers.
The sunlight, zithering their flanks with fire,
Flashes between the shadows as they pass
Barred with electric tremors through the grass
Like wind along the gold strings of a lyre.

Into the flushed air snorting rosy plumes
That smoulder round their feet in drifting fumes,
With dove-like voices call the distant fillies,
While round the herds the stallion wheels his flight,
Engine of beauty volted with delight,
To roll his mare among the trampled lilies.

The Sisters

After hot loveless nights, when cold winds stream
Sprinkling the frost and dew, before the light,
Bored with the foolish things that girls must dream
Because their beds are empty of delight,

Two sisters rise and strip. Out from the night
Their horses run to their low-whistled pleas –
Vast phantom shapes with eyeballs rolling white
That sneeze a fiery steam about their knees:

Through the crisp manes their stealthy prowling hands,
Stronger than curbs, in slow caresses rove,
They gallop down across the milk-white sands
And wade far out into the sleeping cove:

The frost stings sweetly with a burning kiss
As intimate as love, as cold as death:
Their lips, whereon delicious tremors hiss,
Fume with the ghostly pollen of their breath.

Far out on the grey silence of the flood
They watch the dawn in smouldering gyres expand
Beyond them: and the day burns through their blood
Like a white candle through a shuttered hand.

On Some South African Novelists[4]

You praise the firm restraint with which they write
I'm with you there, of course:
They use the snaffle and the curb all right,
But where's the bloody horse?

On the Same

Far from the vulgar haunts of men
Each sits in her "successful room",
Housekeeping with her fountain pen
And writing novels with her broom.

---

[4] This and the next poem, both written in 1926, were attacks on Sarah Gertrude Millin (1889-1968). She responded by putting Campbell into her next novel, *An Artist in the Family* (published 1928), as the ineffectual protagonist, Theo Bissaker.

On Professor Drennan's[5] Verse

Who forced the Muse to this alliance?
A Man of more degrees than parts –
The jilted Bachelor of Science
And Widower of Arts.

Georgian Spring [6]

Who does not love the spring deserves no lovers –
For peaches bloom in Georgia in the spring,
New quarterlies resume their yellow covers,
Anthologies on every bookshelf sing.
The publishers put on their best apparel
To sell the public everything it wants –
A thousand meek soprano voices carol
The loves of homosexuals[7] or plants.
Now let the Old Cow perish, for the tune
Would turn the fatted calf to bully beef:
We know, we know, that "silver is the Moon",
That "skies are blue" was always our belief:
That "grass is green" there can be no denying,
That titled whores in love can be forgot –
All who have heard poor Georgiana[8] sighing

---

[5] C. M. Drennan (1870-1935), professor of English at the University of Witwatersrand, whose poetry and literary judgements provoked Campbell's contempt.

[6] The "Georgian" poets were those who came to prominence during the reign of George V. Campbell, however, uses the word as a term of abuse for those writers whom he associated with Edward Marsh's "Georgian Poetry" anthologies, especially Vita Sackville-West, Sir John Squire, and Marsh himself.

[7] Homosexuality and bisexuality were widespread in the Bloomsbury circle: E.M. Forster, Duncan Grant, J.M. Keynes, Sir Harold Nicolson, Katherine Mansfield, Edward Sackville-West, Vita Sackville-West, James Strachey, Lytton Strachey and Virginia Woolf were all practising homosexuals or bisexuals.

Would think it more surprising were they not:
As for the streams, why, any carp or tench
Could tell you that they "sparkle on their way".
Now for the millionth time the "country wench"
Has lost her reputation "in the hay".
But still the air is full of happy voices,
All bloody: but no matter, let them sing!
For who would frown when all the world rejoices,
And who would contradict when, in the spring,
The English Muse her annual theme rehearses
To tell us birds are singing in the sky?
Only the poet slams the door and curses,
And all the little sparrows wonder why!

From *The Georgiad*

Since Georgians are my theme why should I choose
Any but the most broadly smiling muse?
Inspire me, Fun, and set my fancy gliding,
I'll be your Graves and you my Laura Riding[9],
Or since the metaphor has set you frowning,
That other Robert and his Mrs, Browning.
Let us commune together, soul with soul,
And of our two half-wits compound a whole:
Swap brains with me "for better or for worse"
Till neither knows which writes the other's verse:

---

[8] Vita Sackville-West (1892-1962), aristocrat, poet, novelist and gardener, wife of Sir Harold Nicolson, friend and lover of Virginia Woolf and original of the bisexual hero of Woolf's *Orlando*. Notorious for her insatiable sexual appetite. To Campbell's great distress, she had a brief affair with his wife, Mary.

[9] Robert Graves (1895-1985), important poet, novelist, critic and classical scholar. With Vladimir Nabokov, the most arrogant writer of his generation, according to W.H. Auden (for confirmation of this, see Graves's witty *The Crowning Privilege*). Laura Riding (1901-1991), American poet, critic and prose writer, whose writing remains influential. Graves and Riding were lovers. Graves was later said to have preferred the effects of shell-shock in WWI to living with Laura Riding. Campbell attacked them in a series of articles in 1927 and 1928 for their attempt to impose their critical judgements on a generation of writers.

Think all my thoughts, though they be stale and few,
And when you think I'll think the same as you.
For when "two minds without a single thought,
Two hearts that beat as one," in touch are brought,
There's nothing for it but to burst all fetters
And form a joint Hermaphrodite-of-letters –
A Janus-headed monster, feared of men,
Facing both ways, armed with a double pen,
Able, at once, both to advance and shunt,
To speak behind, and prophesy in front:
A sort of Amphisboena[10], strange to see,
Each with his face where t'other's rump should be:
A quadruped most difficult to class
Though half a man, yet totally an ass...

Now Spring, sweet laxative of Georgian strains,
Quickens the ink in literary veins,
The Stately Homes of England ope their doors
To piping Nancy-boys and crashing Bores,
Where for weekends the scavengers of letters
Convene to chew the fat about their betters –
Over the soup, Shakespeare is put in place,
Wordsworth is mangled with the sole and plaice,
And Milton's glory that once shone so clear
Now with the gravy seems to disappear,
Here Shelley with the orange peel is torn
And Byron's gored by a tame cuckold's horn;
While here ungainly monarchy, annexed
By more ungainly Somebody, is vexed
And turning in her grave exclaims, "What next!
In life did fat and asthma scant my breath,
Then spare me from the Tapeworm[11], Lord, in death."
But now the knives and forks are cleared away
My wanton muse, continuing the day,

---

[10] Double-headed serpent of Greek mythology.
[11] "The Tapeworm" is Lytton Strachey (1880-1932), the controversial critic and biographer.

Summons, from Venus' grove, a moulted dove
To Georgiana's Summer School of Love.
Like some YM and WCA[12]
It welcomes waifs whom love has cast away
A sort of Hostel where we seem to feel
The earnest pulsing of some high ideal –
"Be your own Shakespeare. Step it with the fashion.
Broadcast your love and Pelmanize your Passion.
Our shortcut to the Passions and the Arts –
A correspondence course in seven parts –
Try it! We sterilize our Cupid's darts.
Up-to-date methods: breezy situation:
And only twenty minutes from the station.
Good vegetarian catering. Worth your while!
And furnished in the 'Ye Old Tea Shoppe' style:
The beds are heated up at nine precisely –
And Raymond[13] plays the gramophone so nicely!"
Hither flock all the crowd whom love has wrecked
Of intellectuals without intellect
And sexless folk whose sexes intersect:
All who in Russell's[14] burly frame admire
The "lineaments of gratified desire",
And of despair have baulked the yawning precipice
By swotting up his melancholy recipes
For "happiness" – of which he is the cook
And knows the weight, the flavour, and the look,
Just how much self-control you have to spice it with,
And the right kind of knife you ought to slice it with:
How to "rechauffe" the stock-pot of desire
Although the devil pisses on the fire:
How much long-suffering and how much bonhomie
You must stir up, with patience and economy,

---

[12] "Georgiana's YM and WCA Hostel" was Vita Sackville-West's Kent home, Long Barn.
[13] Raymond Mortimer (1895-1980), distinguished critic and close friend of V. Sackville-West's husband, Sir Harold Nicolson (1886-1968), diplomat, author and journalist.
[14] Bertrand Russell (1872-1970), aristocrat, important philosopher and mathematician; also atheist, political radical and advocate of free love.

To get it right: then of this messy stew
Take the square root, and multiply by two,
And serve lukewarm, before the scum congeals,
An appetizer for your hearth-side meals.
All who have learned this grim felicity
And swotted bliss up, like the Rule of Three,
As if life were a class-examination
And there were penance in cohabitation:
All who of "Happiness" have learned the ropes
From Bertrand Russell or from Marie Stopes[15],
To put their knowledge into practice, some
With fierce determination dour and glum,
But all with earnest faces, hither come...

Though truth be in the Obvious often found,
He scorns to seek it save in things profound:
Far happier with a complicated lie
Than with a simple truth that hits the eye:
Whichever way he goes, his grudging will
Shunts in the opposite direction still,
The intricate is all he does not doubt
And what's through contradictions worried out.
First of earth's protestants, his single voice,
When Eden heard the morning stars rejoice,
Was lifted in complaint: in that loud vote
He struck the first meek English Liberal note:
And in his sluggish vegetarian veins
The spirit of objection still remains,
That sees no fun save in progressive change
Even if it be from normal health to mange.
He roars with agony at Venus' thrill
And takes his pleasures as a bitter pill
Or social duty, much against his will;
And when he leaps enthroned in stallion state,
Less with hot flame, than pedantry, elate,

---

[15] Marie Stopes (1880-1958), feminist and eugenics activist.

Ponders the physiology of birth,
And strives, of sex, "the meaning" to unearth:
And, if he found it, would not stop to breathe
But straight the sex of meaning would unsheathe,
And, even that discovered, would not wait,
But work out its relation to "the State" –
Wasting his life, poor startled fugitive
From life, to find a reason why we live:
Who, even when his weapon's in employ,
Knows not the thundering scalade of joy
When love commanding cries "lay on, MacDuff
And cursed be he who first cries, 'Hold, enough!'"
Who, if he had the power to read and write,
Would fill our Shaws[16] and Russells with delight,
For he, like them, believes that black is white,
Is never sadder than when all goes well
And only could be happy in a Hell:
For with deep broodings and colossal pains
They hatch Utopias from their dusty brains
Which are but Hells, where endless boredom reigns –
Middle-class Hells, built on a cheap, clean plan,
Edens of Abnegation, dread to scan,
Founded upon a universal ban:
For banned from thence is all that fires or thrills,
Pain, vengeance, danger, or the clash of wills –
So vastly greater is their fear of strife
And hate of danger than their love of life:
And Russell's only happiness of mind
(His frail bird's-nest against the boisterous wind
Of living) can be only built and lined
Out of the tearings of his own thin hair
On the foundations of complete despair.
But happiness to a true man will come,
Sometimes, for merely sitting on his bum:

---

[16] George Bernard Shaw (1856-1950), important and enormously influential Anglo-Irish playwright and Fabian Socialist. An unflagging defender of Stalin and Soviet Russia.

And even when we war with mortal spite
There is a joy for ever in the fight.
That's a strange form of happiness that comes
Through being puzzled out of moral sums,
Though Russell thinks his happiness is clear
If, answering to his philosophic leer,
Some milder form of misery appear –
Fool! the disdainful goddess shuns your trap
Who cares for moral virtues not a rap:
Sulla[17] died happy though a lump of vice
And eaten inchmeal by a swarm of lice –
Courage was his, although a rogue heart-whole –
The Ass was foreign to the Roman soul.
Nor knew the Greeks, save in the laughing page,
The philosophic emblem of our age,
Whose Hoof is stamped on all, whose voice is law
Whom every poet serves with reverent awe,
And makes his voice one deafening he-haw,
One loud complaint of devastating griefs
Against his life, his loves, and his beliefs,
Still in his tender disillusion sore
Because, ten years ago, there was a war,
Seeing in all things woes to wound his nerves
Save in the damp philosophy he serves,
Which is the fountain-source of all his woes,
And yet to which the fool for healing goes,
And wonders why he should return all damp
In spirit, with a belly-ful of cramp.
Though living forms buoyed on the surface flow
And all that's dead and rotten sinks below,
These navigators, lubberly and sick,
Sail all by theory – they know the trick –
For truth in obvious things is never found
But only hid in the obscure profound:

---

[17] Lucius Cornelius Sulla (138-78 B.C.), Roman general and dictator, amused himself with actresses on his deathbed.

The well-known capes that on the skyline swerve,
The stars that guide us, and the winds that serve –
At these old fads they never deign to look,
And as for reefs, they are not in the book,
But down below, invisible and dim,
The complexes in soft inertia swim,
Huge useless squids that out of shame or fright
Have sunk insulted from the conscious light –
To these their zigzag courses are related,
By these each ship of fools is navigated:
None with his quadrant ever deigns to sight
The intellect, that sun of fire and light;
And when the ship's piled up, the labour lost,
And all the cargo to the tempest tossed,
They'll blame all things in the revolving year
Save the philosophy by which they steer,
By which they'll prove you, with a final air,
The rock they've split on shouldn't have been there,
And that the world's all wrong whose winds and tides
Don't tally with the tables and the guides;
With pity they regard those hopeless fools
That, ignorant of their preciser rules,
Unscathed upon the rolling billows dance,
And trim their canvas to the winds of chance
And, what's far worse and more benighted still,
Who trust in some slight vestige of free-will
By shortening canvas when the wind's too strong
And keeping watches when the nights are long...

Dinner, most ancient of the Georgian rites,
The noisy prelude of loquacious nights,
At the mere sound of whose unholy gong
The wagging tongue feels resolute and strong,
Senate of bores and parliament of fools,
Where gossip in her native empire rules;
What doleful memories the word suggests –
When I have sat like Job among the guests,

Sandwiched between two bores, a hapless prey,
Chained to my chair, and cannot get away,
Longing, without the appetite to eat,
To fill my ears, more than my mouth, with meat,
And stuff my eardrums full of fish and bread
Against the din to wad my dizzy head:
When I have watched each mouthful that they poke
Between their jaws, and praying they might choke,
Found the descending lump but cleared the way
For further anecdotes and more to say.
O Dinners! take my curse upon you all,
But literary dinners most of all…

Mazeppa[18]

Helpless, condemned, yet still for mercy croaking
Like a trussed rooster swinging by the claws,
They hoisted him: they racked his joints asunder;
They lashed his belly to a thing of thunder –
A tameless brute, with hate and terror smoking,
That never felt the bit between its jaws.

So when his last vain struggle had subsided,
His gleeful butchers wearied of the fun:
Looping the knots about his thighs and back,
With lewd guffaws they heard his sinews crack,
And laughed to see his lips with foam divided,
His eyes too glazed with blood to know the sun.

---

[18] This poem was inspired by Victor Hugo's account of the legend rather than Byron's. Mazeppa was a Polish boy punished for an amorous adventure by being strapped to the back of a wild horse. Rescued by Cossacks, he went on to rule a large empire.

A whip cracked, they were gone: alone they followed
The endless plain: the long day volleyed past
With only the white clouds above them speeding
And the grey steppe into itself receding,
Where each horizon, by a vaster swallowed,
Repeated but the bareness of the last.

Out of his trance he wakened: on they flew:
The blood ran thumping down into his brain:
With skull a-dangle, facing to the sky
That like a great black wind went howling by,
Foaming, he strove to gnash the tethers through
That screwed his flesh into a knot of pain.

To him the earth and sky were drunken things –
Bucked from his senses, jolted to and fro,
He only saw them reeling hugely past,
As sees a sailor soaring at the mast,
Who retches as his sickening orbit swings
The sea above him and the sky below.

Into his swelling veins and open scars
The python cords bit deeper than before
And the great beast, to feel their sharpened sting,
Looping his body in a thunderous sling
As if to jolt his burden to the stars,
Recoiled, and reared, and plunged ahead once more.

Three days had passed, yet could not check nor tire
That cyclone whirling in its spire of sand:
Charged with resounding cordite, as they broke
In sudden flashes through the flying smoke,
The fusillading hoofs in rapid fire
Rumbled a dreary volley through the land.

Now the dark sky with gathering ravens hums:
And vultures, swooping down on his despair,
Struck at the loose and lolling head whereunder
The flying coffin sped, the hearse of thunder,
Whose hoof-beats with the roll of muffled drums
Led on the black processions of the air.

The fourth sun saw the great black wings descending
Where crashed in blood and spume the charger lay:
From the snapped cords a shapeless bundle falls –
Scarce human now, like a cut worm he crawls
Still with a shattered arm his face defending
As inch by inch he drags himself away.

Who'd give a penny for that strip of leather?
Go, set him flapping in a field of wheat,
Or take him as a pull-through for your gun,
Or hang him up to kipper in the sun,
Or leave him here, a strop to hone the weather
And whet the edges of the wind and sleet.

Who on that brow foresees the gems aglow?
Who, in that shrivelled hand, the sword that swings
Wide as a moonbeam through the farthest regions,
To crop the blood-red harvest of the legions,
Making amends to every cheated crow
And feasting vultures on the fat of kings.

This is that Tartar prince, superbly pearled,
Whose glory soon on every wind shall fly,
Whose arm shall wheel the nations into battle,
Whose warcry, rounding up the tribes like cattle,
Shall hurl his cossacks rumbling through the world
As thunder hurls the hail-storm through the sky.

And so it is whenever some new god,
Boastful, and young, and avid of renown,
Would make his presence known upon the earth –
Choosing some wretch from those of mortal birth,
He takes his body like a helpless clod
And on the croup of genius straps it down.

With unseen hand he knots the cord of pain,
Unseen the winged courser strains for flight:
He leads it forth into some peopled space
Where the dull eyes of those who throng the place
See not the wings that wave, the thews that strain,
But only mark the victim of their might.

Left for the passing rabble to admire,
He fights for breath, he chokes, and rolls his eyes:
They mime his agonies with loud guffaws,
They pelt him from the place with muddy paws,
Nor do they hear the sudden snort of fire
To which the tether snaps, the great wings rise...

Vertiginously through the heavens rearing,
Plunging through chasms of eternal pain,
Splendours and horrors open on his view,
And winged fiends like fiercer kites pursue,
With hateful patience at his side careering,
To hook their claws of iron on his brain.

With their green eyes his solitude is starlit,
That lamp the dark and lurk in every brier:
He sinks obscure into the night of sorrow
To rise again, refulgent on the morrow,
With eagles for his ensigns, and the scarlet
Horizon for his Rubicon of fire.

Out of his pain, perhaps, some god-like thing
Is born. A god has touched him, though with whips:
We only know that, hooted from our walls,
He hurtles on his way, he reels, he falls,
And staggers up to find himself a king
With truth a silver trumpet at his lips.

Saint Peter of the Three Canals[19]

(The Fisher's Prayer)

High in his niche above the town,
The three canals with garbage brown,
The rolling waves, and windy dunes –
An old green idol, thunder-scarred,
On whom the spray has crusted hard,
A shell-backed saint, whom time maroons

High stranded on the Rock of Ages,
Of all the ocean-gods and mages
The last surviving Robinson[20] –
Saint Peter-Neptune fronts the wind,
In whose Protean[21] role combined
All deities and creeds are One.

For when the Three-in-One grow thrifty,
Saint Peter, he is One in Fifty,
Saint Peter, he is All in All!
And I have heard the fishers tell
How when from forth the jaws of hell

---

[19] The "three canals" are those that ran through Martigues in Provence, where Campbell lived from 1927-1933.
[20] Crusoe.
[21] After Proteus, the shape-changing water deity of Greek mythology.

No other saint would heed their call,

Doomed wretches at the swamping rowlocks
Have seen a saintly Castor-Pollux[22],
Walking the waves, a burning wraith,
Speed to their aid with strides that quicken
As light as Mother Carey's chicken[23]
Foot-webbed with Mercy and with Faith.

Oh, strong is he when winds are strident
To tame the water with his trident
And bold is he when thunders fly,
And swift – outspeeding as he runs
The corposants[24] of Leda's sons –
To heed the sailor's drowning cry.

By his high tower of creviced rock
The time is always twelve o'clock –
High tower, high time to save our souls!
And hark! his husky bells are calling
By faith and ivy kept from falling
When the night-long mistral rolls.

Deriding Newton,[25] firm and fast,
His crazy tower withstands the blast
A shining miracle to prove –
For all can see, when winds are great,
It needs more faith to keep him straight
Than would a range of mountains move.

---

[22] The warlike twins of Greek mythology; sons of Leda and Zeus, who ravished her in the form of a swan.
[23] A gull.
[24] A corposant: a ball of light sometimes seen on board ship during a storm, St. Elmo's fire (from the Old Spanish, *corpo santo* – holy body).
[25] Sir Isaac Newton (1642-1727), mathematician, physicist, and theorist on subjects ranging from gravity to optics.

Around him float on airy sculls
Bright angels in the form of gulls
His seaward messages to go:
Deep in his bosom nest the doves
In token of seraphic loves,
To keep his garments-white as snow.

Archbishop of the deep-sea Tritons,
When round his head the glory lightens,
Mitred by the moon with flame,
Safe in the harbour that he guards
The masts, adoring, lift their yards
The signal of the cross to frame.

Among the clouds his feet are set,
And in his hands the spangled net
Where souls of men, as small red fish
Smoked with spindrift, soused in spray,
And salted till the Judgement Day,
Await the great Millennial Dish.

Amphibious saint, crustacean idol,
At once celestial and tidal,
To his bland creed all doubt atones –
Where Dagon[26] weds with Mother Carey,
Jehovah wooes a Mermaid Mary,
And Thetis sins with Davey Jones.

Arch-patriarch of Navigation,
He bears the lifebuoy of Salvation
To souls that flounder in the lurch:
With God he walks the azure decks,
Great Quartermaster-Pontifex
Whose vessel is the Holy Church.

---

[26] Philistine idol.

Her sails are swelled with hymns, her spars
Are pulleyed with the moon and stars
From which depend, a hardy gang,
Her crew of human fears and hopes –
And metaphysics are the ropes
By which those desperadoes hang.

Her ropes with love and faith are spliced,
Her compass is the Cross of Christ,
Pointing the quarters of the world,
And her auxiliary steam
The vapour of the prophet's dream
To waft her when the winds are furled.

With track of fire she cleaves the distance,
To genuflexions of her pistons
The rapture of the turbine rolls:
Her stokehold is the deep Avernus[27]
Where Satan feeds the roaring furnace
And sinners are the burning coals...

O Captain of the Saint-filled Ark,
Ere loaded to the Plimsoll mark
Your saintly cargo put to sea,
And we attend the Great Inspection,
The roll-call of the Resurrection,
The pay-day of Eternity –

Remember in your high promotion
How once, poor flotsam of the Ocean,
You followed such a trade as mine.
The winter nights, have you forgotten,
When hauling on a seine as rotten
You cracked your knuckles on the line?

---

[27] Volcanic Italian lake: in mythology, the entrance to the underworld.

Have you forgot the cramp that clinches
Your shoulder, turning at the winches –
And not a mullet in the mesh?
Have you forgotten Galilee –
The night you floundered in the sea
Because your faith was in your flesh?

Be with me, then, when nights are lone
And from the pampas of the Rhône,
Thrilling with sleet, the great guns blow:
When the black mistral roars avenging
Increase the horse-power of my engine,
Hallow my petrol ere I go!

The Albatross

Stretching white wings in strenuous repose,
Sleeving them in the silver frills of sleep,
As I was carried, far from other foes,
To shear the long horizons of the deep,

A swift ship struck me down: through gusty glooms
I spun from fierce collision with her spars:
Shrill through the sleety pallor of my plumes
Whistled the golden bullets of the stars:

Loose on the gale my shattered wreck was strewn
And, conquered by the envious winds at last,
A rag upon the red horns of the moon,
Was tossed and gored and trampled by the blast.

Flapping the water like a sodden flag,
No more to rise, shot down by stormy guns,
How shamefully these great sprained sinews drag

That bracketed my purpose with the sun's ...

To the dark ocean I had dealt my laws
And when the shores rolled by, their speed was mine:
The ranges moved like long two-handed saws
Notching the scarlet west with jagged line:

Swerved like a thin blue scythe, and smoothly reaping
Their mushroom minarets and toadstool towers,
My speed had set the steel horizon sweeping
And razed the Indies like a field of flowers:

Feathered with palm and eyed with broad lagoons,
Fanned open to the dimly-burning sky,
A peacock-train of fierce mesmeric moons,
The coast of Africa had rustled by:

The broad curve of the west, with nightward tilt,
Wheeled down, and nations stood upon their crowns:
Each tower a crutch, each chimney-stack a stilt,
Across the nether sky, their fog-red towns

Went striding – while up far opposing seas
I by earth's sunward wheel was steeply borne
To see the green foam-heaved antipodes
Capsize their thousand islands on the morn.

Then through the gloom wherein, like tiny spiders
Webbed in their flimsy rays, the systems spawn,
Up dim blue rocks of cloud, with scarlet fibres,
Crawled the gigantic lichens of the dawn;

Striped with the fiery colours of the sky,
Tigered with war-paint, ramping as they rolled,
The green waves charged the sunrise letting fly
Their porpoises like boomerangs of gold.

Exploding from white cotton-pods of cloud
I saw the tufted gulls before me blow,
The black cape-hens beneath me, and the proud
White gannet in his catapult of snow.

The cliff-ringed islands where the penguins nest
Sheltered their drowsy legions from the foam
When evening brought the cormorants to rest,
Gondolas of the tempest, steering home:

To sleep or cackle, grouped in homely rings,
I left them roosting warm in their own dung,
And while they fattened there, with homeless wings
The great harp of the hurricanes I strung:

Towering far up amid the red star-sockets,
I saw deep down, in vast flotillas shoaled,
The phosphorescent whales, like bursting rockets,
Bore through the gloom their long ravines of gold.

Far coral islands rose in faint relief
Each with its fringe of palms and shut lagoon,
Where, with a running fuse of spray, the reef
Set off the golden crackers of the moon.

By nameless capes, where the slow thunder prowls,
I dared the shapeless phantoms of the night,
Relentless as the noon to dazzled owls,
Inflicting beauty on their hate of light.

Squelching like sodden shoes, with canvas trailing,
Doomed vessels swung their teetering yards on high,
Or downward as they plunged, with syrens wailing,
Reared to the stars their tempest-throttled cry.

I read my doom in those great shattered ribs
Nor with vague fancies drugged my truth-of-sight,
I knew the stars for momentary squibs
In the perpetual horror of the night:

I saw how vile a thing it is to die
Save when careering on their sunward course,
The strong heart cracks, the shivered senses fly,
Stunned by their own expenditure of force.

Erect, unterrified, though robbed of breath,
In those wild hours of triumph had I died,
The shades around, as in a meteor's death,
Had seen annihilation glorified.

My stiff quills made the hurricane their lyre
Where, pronged with azure flame, the black rain streams:
Huge brindled shadows barred with gloomy fire
Prowling the red horizon of my dreams,

Thick storm-clouds threatened me with dense eclipse,
The wind made whirling towels of the stars-
Over black waves where sky-careering ships
Gibbet the moon upon their crazy spars,

From bow-bent wings I shot my white resilience
Grazing the tempest like a shaft of light,
Till with the sunrise, shivering into trillions
Of winged fish, I saw the wave ignite.

Through calms that seemed the swoon of all the gales,
On snowy frills that softest winds had spun,
I floated like a seed with silken sails
Out of the sleepy thistle of the sun.

I had been dashed in the gold spray of dawns,
And hit with silver by the stars' faint light,
The red moon charged at me with lowered horns,
Buffalo-shouldered by the gloom of night:

Broidering earth's senseless matter with my sight,
Weaving my life around it like a robe,
Onward I draw my silken clues of flight,
Spooled by the wheeling glories of the globe.

The globe, revolving like a vast cocoon,
Unwound its threading leagues at my desire:
With burning stitches by the sun and moon
My life was woven like a shawl of fire.

Clashing the surf-white fringe that round it runs,
Its giant mesh of fire-shot silk, unfurled
And braided with a chain of flashing suns,
Fleeces the craggy shoulders of the world:

How dimly now its threads are ravelled out,
Its gorgeous colours smoulder from my brain,
While my numbed memory, the world about,
Rays forth its thin meridians of pain.

My eyes with wild funereal trophies blaze
Like dying torches – spoils of azure nights
And the slain suns my speed has shorn of rays
And dashed to bleed upon the western heights.

Night surges up the black reef of the world,
Shaking the skies in ponderous collapse,
I hear the long horizons, steeply hurled,
Rush cataracting down through starless gaps.

No more to rise, the last sun bombs the deep
And strews my shattered senses with its light –
My spirit knows the silence it must keep
And with the ocean hankers for the night.

Tristan da Cunha

Snore in the foam; the night is vast and blind;
The blanket of the mist about your shoulders,
Sleep your old sleep of rock, snore in the wind,
Snore in the spray! the storm your slumber lulls,
His wings are folded in your nest of boulders
As on their eggs the grey wings of your gulls.

No more as when, so dark an age ago,
You hissed a giant cinder from the ocean,
Around your rocks you furl the shawling snow
Half sunk in your own darkness, vast and grim,
And round you on the deep with surly motion
Pivot your league-long shadow as you swim.

Why should you haunt me thus but that I know
My surly heart is in your own displayed,
Round whom such leagues in endless circuit flow,
Whose hours in such a gloomy compass run –
A dial with its league-long arm of shade
Slowly revolving to the moon and sun.

My pride has sunk, like your grey fissured crags,
By its own strength o'ertoppled and betrayed:
I, too, have burned the wind with fiery flags
Who now am but a roost for empty words,

An island of the sea whose only trade
Is in the voyages of its wandering birds.
Did you not, when your strength became your pyre,
Deposed and tumbled from your flaming tower,
Awake in gloom from whence you sank in fire,
To find, Antaeus[28]-like, more vastly grown,
A throne in your own darkness, and a power
Sheathed in the very coldness of your stone?

Your strength is that you have no hope or fear,
You march before the world without a crown,
The nations call you back, you do not hear,
The cities of the earth grow grey behind you,
You will be there when their great flames go down
And still the morning in the van will find you.

You march before the continents, you scout
In front of all the earth; alone you scale
The mast-head of the world, a lorn look-out,
Waving the snowy flutter of your spray
And gazing back in infinite farewell
To suns that sink and shores that fade away.

From your grey tower what long regrets you fling
To where, along the low horizon burning,
The great swan-breasted seraphs soar and sing,
And suns go down, and trailing splendours dwindle,
And sails on lonely errands unreturning
Glow with a gold no sunrise can rekindle.

Turn to the night; these flames are not for you
Whose steeple for the thunder swings its bells;
Grey Memnon[29], to the tempest only true,
Turn to the night, turn to the shadowing foam,

---

[28] Giant of Greek mythology who gained strength from contact with the earth. He died when Hercules lifted him in the air and crushed him.
[29] A colossal statue of Pharaoh Amenhotep III near Thebes that was reputed to give out a musical note when touched by the rays of the morning sun.

And let your voice, the saddest of farewells,
With sullen curfew toll the grey wings home.
The wind, your mournful syren, haunts the gloom;
The rocks, spray-clouded, are your signal guns
Whose stony nitre, puffed with flying spume,
Rolls forth in grim salute your broadside hollow
Over the gorgeous burials of suns
To sound the tocsin of the storms that follow.

Plunge forward like a ship to battle hurled,
Slip the long cables of the failing light,
The level rays that moor you to the world:
Sheathed in your armour of eternal frost,
Plunge forward, in the thunder of the fight
To lose yourself as I would fain be lost.

Exiled like you and severed from my race
By the cold ocean of my own disdain,
Do I not freeze in such a wintry space,
Do I not travel through a storm as vast
And rise at times, victorious from the main,
To fly the sunrise at my shattered mast?

Your path is but a desert where you reap
Only the bitter knowledge of your soul:
You fish with nets of seaweed in the deep
As fruitlessly as I with nets of rhyme –
Yet forth you stride, yourself the way, the goal,
The surges are your strides, your path is time.

Hurled by what aim to what tremendous range!
A missile from the great sling of the past,
Your passage leaves its track of death and change
And ruin on the world: you fly beyond
Leaping the current of the ages vast
As lightly as a pebble skims a pond.

The years are undulations in your flight
Whose awful motion we can only guess –
Too swift for sense, too terrible for sight,
We only know how fast behind you darken
Our days like lonely beacons of distress:
We know that you stride on and will not harken.

Now in the eastern sky the fairest planet
Pierces the dying wave with dangled spear,
And in the whirring hollows of your granite
That vaster sea to which you are a shell
Sighs with a ghostly rumour, like the drear
Moan of the nightwind in a hollow cell.

We shall not meet again; over the wave
Our ways divide, and yours is straight and endless,
But mine is short and crooked to the grave:
Yet what of these dark crowds amid whose flow
I battle like a rock, aloof and friendless,
Are not their generations vague and endless
The waves, the strides, the feet on which I go?

Horses on the Camargue[30]
(To A. F. Tschiffely[31])

In the grey wastes of dread,
The haunt of shattered gulls where nothing moves
But in a shroud of silence like the dead,
I heard a sudden harmony of hooves,
And, turning, saw afar
A hundred snowy horses unconfined,
The silver runaways of Neptune's car
Racing, spray-curled, like waves before the wind.
Sons of the Mistral, fleet
As him with whose strong gusts they love to flee,
Who shod the flying thunders on their feet
And plumed them with the snortings of the sea;
Theirs is no earthly breed
Who only haunt the verges of the earth
And only on the sea's salt herbage feed –
Surely the great white breakers gave them birth.
For when for years a slave,
A horse of the Camargue, in alien lands,
Should catch some far-off fragrance of the wave
Carried far inland from his native sands,
Many have told the tale[32]
Of how in fury, foaming at the rein,
He hurls his rider; and with lifted tail,
With coal-red eyes and cataracting mane,
Heading his course for home,
Though sixty foreign leagues before him sweep,
Will never rest until he breathes the foam

---

[30]"*Camargue*: Pampa at the mouth of the Rhône which together with the Sauvage and the desert Crau form a vast grazing ground for thousands of wild cattle and horses. The Camarguais horses are a distinct race." – Campbell's note.

[31] Aimé Felix Tschiffely, famous horseman and author of *Tschiffely's Ride*, was a friend of Campbell's in London until his death in 1954.

[32] "*Trident*: dual allusion to the trident of Neptune and that carried by the guardians or cowboys of the Camargue." – Campbell's note.

And hears the native thunder of the deep.
But when the great gusts rise
And lash their anger on these and coasts,
When the scared gulls career with mournful cries
And whirl across the waste like driven ghosts:
When hail and fire converge,
The only souls to which they strike no pain
Are the white-crested fillies of the surge
And the white horses of the windy plain.
Then in their strength and pride
The stallions of the wilderness rejoice;
They feel their Master's trident in their side,
And high and shrill they answer to his voice.
With white tails smoking free,
Long streaming manes, and arching necks, they show
Their kinship to their sisters of the sea –
And forward hurl their thunderbolts of snow.
Still out of hardship bred,
Spirits of power and beauty and delight
Have ever on such frugal pastures fed
And loved to course with tempests through the night.

Mass at Dawn

I dropped my sail and dried my dripping seines
Where the white quay is chequered by cool planes
In whose great branches, always out of sight,
The nightingales are singing day and night.
Though all was grey beneath the moon's grey beam,
My boat in her new paint shone like a bride,
And silver in my baskets shone the bream:
My arms were tired and I was heavy-eyed,
But when with food and drink, at morning-light,
The children met me at the water-side,
Never was wine so red or bread so white.

Autumn

I love to see, when leaves depart,
The clear anatomy arrive,
Winter, the paragon of art,
That kills all forms of life and feeling
Save what is pure and will survive.

Already now the clanging chains
Of geese are harnessed to the moon:
Stripped are the great sun-clouding planes:
And the dark pines, their own revealing,
Let in the needles of the noon.

Strained by the gale the olives whiten
Like hoary wrestlers bent with toil
And, with the vines, their branches lighten
To brim our vats where summer lingers
In the red froth and sun-gold oil.

Soon on our hearth's reviving pyre
Their rotted stems will crumble up:
And like a ruby, panting fire,
The grape will redden on your fingers
Through the lit crystal of the cup.

Choosing a Mast[33]

This mast, new-shaved, through whom I rive the ropes,
Says she was once an oread[34] of the slopes,
Graceful and tall upon the rocky highlands,
A slender tree as vertical as noon,

---

[33] The poem reflects Campbell's experience in Provence of shaping a new mast for his boat "La Clemence".
[34] A tree-nymph.

And her low voice was lovely as the silence
Through which a fountain whistles to the moon,
Who now of the white spray must take the veil
And, for her songs, the thunder of the sail.

I chose her for her fragrance, when the spring
With sweetest resins swelled her fourteenth ring
And with live amber welded her young thews:
I chose her for the glory of the Muse,
Smoother of forms, that her hard-knotted grain,
Grazed by the chisel, shaven by the plane,
Might from the steel as cool a burnish take
As from the bladed moon a windless lake.

I chose her for her eagerness of flight
Where she stood tiptoe on the rocky height
Lifted by her own perfume to the sun,
While through her rustling plumes with eager sound
Her eagle spirit, with the gale at one,
Spreading wide pinions, would have spurned the ground
And her own sleeping shadow, had they not
With thymy fragrance charmed her to the spot.

Lover of song, I chose this mountain pine
Not only for the straightness of her spine
But for her songs: for there she loved to sing
Through a long noon's repose of wave and wing,
The fluvial swirling of her scented hair
Sole rill of song in all that windless air,
And her slim form the naiad of the stream
Afloat upon the languor of its theme;

And for the soldier's fare on which she fed:
Her wine the azure, and the snow her bread;
And for her stormy watches on the height,
For only out of solitude or strife
Are born the sons of valour and delight;

And lastly for her rich, exulting life,
That with the wind stopped not its singing breath
But carolled on, the louder for its death.

Under a pine, when summer days were deep,
We loved the most to lie in love or sleep:
And when in long hexameters the west
Rolled his grey surge, the forest for his lyre,
It was the pines that sang us to our rest,
Loud in the wind and fragrant in the fire,
With legioned voices swelling all night long,
From Pelion[35] to Provence, their storm of song.

It was the pines that fanned us in the heat,
The pines, that cheered us in the time of sleet,
For which sweet gifts I set one dryad free;
No longer to the wind a rooted foe,
This nymph shall wander where she longs to be
And with the blue north wind arise and go,
A silver huntress with the moon to run
And fly through rainbows with the rising sun;

And when to pasture in the glittering shoals
The guardian mistral drives his thundering foals,
And when like Tartar horsemen racing free
We ride the snorting fillies of the sea,
My pine shall be the archer of the gale
While on the bending willow curves the sail
From whose great bow the long keel shooting home
Shall fly, the feathered arrow of the foam.

---

[35] Mountain in Thessaly.

Posada[36]

Outside, it froze. On rocky arms
Sleeping face-upwards to the sun
Lay Spain. Her golden hair was spun
From sky to sky. Her mighty charms
Breathed soft beneath her robe of farms
And gardens: while her snowy breasts,
Sierras white, with crimson crests,
Were stained with sunset. At the Inn,
A priest, a soldier, and a poet
(Fate-summoned, though they didn't know it)
Met there, a shining hour to win.
A song, a blessing, and a grin
Were melted in one cup of mirth,
The Eternal Triumvirs of Earth
Foresaw their golden age begin.

Driving Cattle to Casas Buenas[37]

The roller perched upon the wire,
Telegrams running through his toes,
At my approach would not retire
But croaked a greeting as he rose,
A telegraph of solar fire.
Girth-high the poppies and the daisies
To brush the belly of my mule:
The thyme was smoking up God's praises,
The sun was warm, the wind was cool,
The white sierra was the icy
Refrigerator of that noon
And in that air so fresh, so spicy,

---

[36] Inn (Spanish).
[37] A village near Toledo.

So steep, so pale, Toledo's June,
The sun seemed smaller than the moon.
Wading through seas of fire and blood
(I never saw such flowers before)
I said to Apis, "What a cud
To make the bulls of Bashan roar!"
The church, with storks upon the steeple,
And scarcely could my cross be signed,
When round me came those Christian people
So hospitably clean, and kind.
Beans and Alfalfa in the manger –
Alfalfa, there was never such!
And rice and rabbit for the stranger.
Thank you very much!

From *Mithraic Emblems*:[38]

The Seven Swords[39]

Of seven hues in white elision,[40]
the radii of your silver gyre,
are the seven swords of vision
that spoked the prophets' flaming tyre;
their sistered stridences ignite
the spectrum of the poets' lyre
whose unison becomes a white
revolving disc of stainless fire,
and sights the eye of that sole star
that, in the heavy clods we are,
the kindred seeds of fire can spy,
or, in the cold shell of the rock,
the red yolk of the phoenix-cock
whose feathers in the meteors fly.

---

[38] Campbell had become interested in the dead and mysterious worship of Mithras in Provence, which he saw as a precursor of Christianity. See Introduction.

[39] Inspired by a devotional image of Our Lady of Sorrows in a church in Provence.

[40] "The seven colours of the rainbow when painted on a swiftly revolving disc combine to form the purest whiteness." – Campbell's note.

From *Mithraic Emblems*:

The Morning

The woods have caught the singing flame
in live bouquets of loveliest hue –
the scarlet fink, the chook, the sprew,
that seem to call me by my name.
Such friendship, understanding, truth,
this morning from its Master took
as if San Juan de la Cruz [41]
had written it in his own book,
and went on reading it aloud
until his voice was half the awe
with which this loneliness is loud,
and every word were what I saw
live, shine, or suffer in that Ray
whose only shadow is our day.

---

[41] Saint John of the Cross (1542-1591): Spanish Carmelite, poet, mystic and Doctor of the Church.

From *Mithraic Emblems*:

San Juan[42] Sings

– As if San Juan sang aloud
until his song became whatever
drew my sight: the sailing cloud:
the Sea that rushes on forever,
and the Sun that makes it proud:
the blue wind tethered to the tree
grazing the poppies by my side –
the wind so blue you cannot see,
so light and swift you cannot ride!
the City White, above the air,
(the City where I long to go)
and the sunbeams playing there
as windblown threads of golden hair
are scattered on a nape of snow.

From *Mithraic Emblems*:

Mithras Speaks 1

"A flitting rainbow is your life,
your body but a passing cloud,
remember this when you are proud
or when you look upon a knife."
(He said) "We work for the same Boss
though you are earth and I a star,
and herdsmen both, though my guitar
is strung to strum the world across!

---

[42] Saint John of the Cross.

as if you'd known me all your life
go with good luck as with a wife;
though there's a line you may not cross
you will not find it in this land
and you can sleep on this kaross"[43]
(He stroked the meadow with his hand).

From *Mithraic Emblems*:

Mithras Speaks 2

"The World put down its lovely mane,
your fathers stroked it with their ships;
they won you, with their guns and whips,
the huge hosanna of the plain.
Through the lush lilies as you crash
and rein horizons in your hold,
while, baying fire, the aloes slash
your stirrups with their fangs of gold –
Sing, Cowboy! string your strong guitar!
For each Vaquero is a star
and Abel's sons the line will cross,
under the stretched, terrific wings,
the outspread arms (our soaring King's) –
the man they made an Albatross!"

---

[43] "Kaross: A rug made of the fur or of the fleeces of antelopes, otters or leopards." – Campbell's note.

To the Sun[44]

Oh let your shining orb grow dim,
Of Christ the mirror and the shield,
That I may gaze through you to Him,
See half the miracle revealed,
And in your seven hues behold
The Blue Man walking on the Sea;
The Green, beneath the summer tree,
Who called the children; then the Gold,
With palms; the Orange, flaring bold
With scourges; Purple in the garden
(As Greco[45] saw): and then the Red
Torero (Him who took the toss
And rode the black horns of the cross –
But rose snow-silver from the dead!)

The Fight

One silver-white and one of scarlet hue,
Storm-hornets humming in the wind of death,
Two aeroplanes were fighting in the blue
Above our town; and if I held my breath,
It was because my youth was in the Red
While in the White an unknown pilot flew –
And that the White had risen overhead.

From time to time the crackle of a gun
Far into flawless ether faintly railed,
And now, mosquito-thin, into the Sun,
And now like mating dragonflies they sailed:

---

[44] "'To the Sun': This was the last poem of *Mithraic Emblems*, but I judged it better to separate it." – Campbell's note.
[45] El Greco, (1541-1614), Spanish painter of Greek origin, famous for his religious paintings, in which he often made much use of the colour purple.

And, when like eagles near the earth they drove,
The Red, still losing what the White had won,
The harder for each lost advantage strove.

So lovely lay the land – the towers and trees
Taking the seaward counsel of the stream:
The city seemed, above the far-off seas,
The crest and turret of a Jacob's dream[46],
And those two gun-birds in their frantic spire

At death-grips for its ultimate regime –
Less to be whirled by anger than desire.

Till (Glory!) from his chrysalis of steel
The Red flung wide the fatal fans of fire:
I saw the long flames, ribboning, unreel,
And slow bitumen trawling from his pyre.
I knew the ecstasy, the fearful throes,
And the white phoenix from his scarlet sire,
As silver in the Solitude he rose.

The towers and trees were lifted hymns of praise,
The city was a prayer, the land a nun:
The noonday azure strumming all its rays
Sang that a famous battle had been won,
As signing his white Cross, the very Sun,
The Solar Christ and captain of my days
Zoomed to the zenith; and his will was done.

---

[46] A reference to Genesis 28, in which Jacob has a vision of angels ascending and descending a ladder between heaven and earth, and is promised a multitude of descendants to inherit the Holy Land.

To "the Future"

You all-propitious season,
Older than Adam's race –
With what foresight and reason
You shame to show your face!

Toledo, July 1936[47]

Toledo, when I saw you die
And heard the roof of Carmel[48] crash,
A spread-winged phoenix from its ash
The Cross remained against the sky!
With horns of flame and haggard eye
The mountain vomited with blood,
A thousand corpses down the flood
Were rolled gesticulating by,
And high above the roaring shells
I heard the silence of your bells
Who've left these broken stones behind
Above the years to make your home,
And burn, with Athens and with Rome,
A sacred city of the mind.

---

[47] Campbell was caught up in the fighting in Toledo at the outbreak of the Spanish Civil War, as this and the following poems attest.
[48] The Carmelite priory above Campbell's Toledo house was burned, and the friars shot by communist militiamen at the outbreak of the civil war.

Hot Rifles

Our rifles were too hot to hold,
The night was made of tearing steel,
And down the street the volleys rolled
Where as in prayer the snipers kneel.
From every cranny, rift, or creek,
I heard the fatal furies scream,
And the moon held the river's gleam
Like a long rifle to its cheek.
Of all that fearful fusillade
I reckoned not the gain or loss
To see (her every forfeit paid)
And grander, though her riches fade,
Toledo, hammered on the Cross,
And in her Master's wounds arrayed.

Christ in Uniform

Close at my side a girl and boy
Fell firing, in the doorway here,
Collapsing with a strangled cheer
As on the very couch of joy,
And onward through a wall of fire
A thousand others rolled the surge,
And where a dozen men expire
A hundred myrmidons emerge –
As if the Christ, our Solar Sire,
Magnificent in their intent,
Returned the bloody way he went,
Of so much blood, of such desire,
And so much valour proudly spent,
To weld a single heart of fire.

The Alcazar Mined[49]

This Rock of Faith, the thunder-blasted –
Eternity will hear it rise
With those who (Hell itself out-lasted)
Will lift it with them to the skies!
Till whispered through the depths of Hell
The censored Miracle be known,
And flabbergasted Fiends re-tell
How fiercer tortures than their own
By living faith were overthrown;
How mortals, thinned to ghastly pallor,
Gangrened and rotting to the bone,
With winged souls of Christian valour
Beyond Olympus or Valhalla
Can heave ten thousand tons of stone!

---

[49] During the siege of the Alcazar by the Republicans in Toledo (20 July-27 September 1936), the besiegers made several attempts to blow up the fortress; they destroyed it but without quelling the resistance, which continued in the ruins.

To My Jockey[50]

Killed at my side by the shock troops, Toledo, March 16

For the Guitar

I never felt such glory
As handcuffs on my wrists,
My body stunned and gory
And toothmarks on my fists,
The triumph through the square
(My horse behind me led),
A pistol at my cutlets,
Three rifles at my head.
And four of those black bastards[51]
To hold a single man:
And four to take him to the gaol –
Proclaiming thus my clan.
Through the great grill I saw
Our other horse had fled
With empty saddle: then I knew,
"Mosquito", you were dead!
And down along the mesa
The sun was swirling red –
To show that Death is royal,
As royal as our Life
(You took it as a mistress,
I'll take it as a wife).
There's a black Virgin,
There's a gypsy Christ
Out of whose wounds are pouring
The gouts that make me wise.
And there's the black Saint Sarah[52]

---

[50] The "jockey" was a gypsy, "Mosquito" Lozoya, who did odd jobs for Campbell. "The reason why the author was able to bury the gypsy was that the total amnesty, telegraphed two hours after his arrest, freed him." – Campbell's note.

[51] "*Black bastards*: Guardias de Asalto." – Campbell's note.

That lives beside the Sea
And prays for each vaquero
The same as you or me.
I lift you like a coney,
Collect your scattered tripes,
Wrap round the gay horse-blanket
(Like you, all scarlet stripes),
I bury you brave gypsy –
You only had your knife!
In death collect the pleasure
That I collect in life.
I too am friends with danger
And to salute the brave
I'll stand up, though a stranger,
The cypress on your grave.

The Carmelites of Toledo[53]

Of the two Camps[54], from the beginning,
And long before their tides were hurled,
I knew which would do all the winning
If not as most regards the world,
Though earthly victory might come
As so much backwash, drift, or scum
Its sky-careering wave uncurled.

For in the City built with prayer
The Masters of the joyful science
Had held the ages in defiance,

---

[52] "*Saint Sarah*: The Gypsy Saint of Saintes Maries at the mouth of the Rhône." – Campbell's note.
[53] See "Toledo, July, 1936." These poems deal with an incident during the Spanish Civil War in which the Carmelite priory above the Campbells' house was burned and seventeen Carmelite friars were shot by communist militiamen.
[54] The Spanish Republicans and Nationalists.

Whose only study is to dare,
Who hardest on the anvil deal,
And thrive upon the hardest fare
Of all who work in fire and steel.

Their lives had won, at comfort's price,
The temper that Toledo lords,
Over a world of waving swords,
From fierce extremes of fire and ice
Deriving such an edge and brilliance
That to their lightning and resilience
No earthly conquest could suffice.

They sailed upon a sinking deck
Beneath a single Mast and Spar
To colonize this blood-red star
Where states and empires plunge to wreck
And, with the world for their Peru,
To vanquish more with wound and scar
Than ever sword set out to do.

No soul so creeping beneath scorn
But they could file its rankled fetters:
Bawds, drunkards, pimps, and men of letters
Who wish their abject souls unborn,
Subjected to their living radium
Returned, as athletes to the stadium,
Who'd come on creaking stretchers borne.

I did not come to dump my sins,
Which, stronger than a mule, I carried,
To their foul load so blithely married
They could not bring me to my shins
For any trick of thief or strumpet.
I came because I heard the Trumpet
When the mad victory begins!

So a loud ass, to be admired,
With no persuasion from the quirt
And heedless that his load is dirt,
By his own braying pibroch-fired,
Might leap the gate, and brave the scoffer,
And come his services to offer
Where snow-white chargers are required.

But from such eagle towers of pity
Eusebio[55] heard my drab confession
That rumbled like a Red procession
When to the "Meeting" roars the City
With lifted fist and lungs that bray,
His looks abashed that loud Committee
And sent them muttering on their way.

There, parted from those pistoleros,
I stood alone with what I am
As by a wrecked and burning tram.
The companies of drunken heroes
Whose valour varies with their numbers,
Dispersing, teetered to their slumbers,
And each as harmless as a lamb.

And though their fate I could resist,
That gallowed every workless wreck
To dangle from his lifted fist,
His arm a hangrope to his neck,
When like a clinical exhibit
The gesture of the Walking Gibbet
Has jerked him for the Jews to peck –

---

[55] "One of the Carmelite friars in the Friary of Toledo and Campbell's confessor, who gave himself to the Red Mob in the hope of saving the inmates of the house." (Note at the head of the poem when published in *The Tablet*, 1 January, 1938.)

Yet, to be pitied from such height,
I felt what whets the frenzy-cursed
To slay these Witnesses the first,
Whose cold-and-hunger-bearing sprite,
To thrice their injuries resigned,
Reproaches and rebukes them worst
For so babooning from their kind:

Which, like a glass in a dark place,
Being so much in league with Light,
Might, glinting on the murderer's face,
Reveal him to his own affright,
Or, with a shimmer on the dirk,
Deflect it from the kind of work
That slinks, offended, from the sight.

Their Church, though poorer than an attic,
Anachronized, and seemed to void
Of meaning all that's Meetingoid,
Or tries to pass for Democratic –
More than the grievances they roar,
Its silence galled them to the core
That was so ageless and ecstatic!

But soon the Hoopoe[56], changing score,
The crested harbinger of battle,
That shares our life amongst the cattle
And only sings in times of war,
The corposant of coming slaughter,
Was singing by the blood-red water
As scarce in centuries before.

---

[56] Spanish peasants regarded the hoopoe as a bird of ill-omen.

And Nature never lit that shore
Where ghost-white suns, foreboding, sank.
And, mirrored with our horses, drank
The flames of blood and liquid ore,
Where Tagus[57] showed that Sky of skies
To which so many soon would rise,
With flames for feathers, streaming gore.

By every sign the times were known,
Humanity by day benighted,
The flesh defiled, dominion slighted,
Blasphemed the high, majestic throne,
And on each wind the whisper blown –
"The weak are strong in hate united,
Woe to the strong who ride alone!"

To those of Carmel half a stranger,
Their purchase from the farms I'd brought
With veld-flowers as an afterthought
That seemed too lovely for the manger,
And now, when ruin lit the towers,
Beset by death, and tracked with danger,
I could not break that chain of flowers:

But proudlier rode to their doomed door
Than ever, plumed and spurred, before
To thundering pigeon-flights of hands,
When, snowed with talc, cascading pearls,
And forested with jet-blue curls,
A whole Sierra made of girls
Sheered sunward from the bloodlit sands!

---

[57] River which flows around Toledo and enters the sea at Lisbon.

But Nero's Circus[58] would have been as
A play, himself a paltry showman,
To this most awful of arenas
That stretched, Sahara to the Roman,
With half-a-million lives to spill,
Where to the howl of worse hyenas
I rode but as an alguazil[59].

The Carmelites, all terror quelled,
The first of the toreros came
In "clothes of light"[60] whose ghostly flame
Was only of the soul beheld,
To flaunt their crimson one by one:
And Death, in turn, by each was felled
Till valour seemed to fix the sun.

The Taurine[61] Sun, in trancèd swoon,
Who loves to linger over peril
And late through evening skies of beryl
Will stretch a famous afternoon,
Had hung so long upon their valour
As, when the smoke dissolved in pallor,
To seem the chill, belated moon.

His radiant face when last I saw
Eusebio bade me take delight:
His flesh was flame, his blood its light
That sought the fire as fire the straw,
And of his agony so cruel
As ruthlessly devoured the spite
As eager flame devours the fuel.

---

[58] A reference to the persecutions of the Christians in the Circus Maximus during the reign of the Roman emperor Nero.
[59] Minor official in a Spanish bullring.
[60] Translation of the Spanish *traje de luces* worn by bullfighters.
[61] A reference to Mithraism. Key adjuncts to Mithras were the bull and the sun.

Small wonder then as trash too earthly
The gunbutts drove me from the pin
They smashed to let such Princes in,
When, too presumptuous, as unworthy,
My carcase for a Crown to barter,
The blows acceding to the Martyr
Rebuffed me for a Harlequin.[62]

In my black mask, with bleeding eyes,
I woke as one for gala dressed,
My scapular beneath my vest
Which only then I learned to prize,
And there, like Romeo, the mad lover,
In the forbidden town, discover
And hold the Loved-One to my breast.

So tenderly to fall enamoured[63]
So late – Oh, what a fool was I
To blunder ignorantly by
Just when the third great Nail was hammered,
The strident spear had gashed the cry,
When dicers for the leavings clamoured,
And blood was streaming down the sky!

The Flood-rush, with their blood to break it,
Now filled the land with fire and slaughter.
The Tagus, that was running water,
Was now alive, if blood could make it
That had not had the time to die:
The town, if rushing flames could take it
Was half rebuilded in the sky –

---

[62] This stanza refers to a beating Campbell received at the hands of the Assault Guards on 16 March 1936.
[63] Campbell's language here (and elsewhere in this poem) is a direct echo of the poems of Saint John of the Cross.

As now a lunar landscape tells
With craters for its domes and spires,
The architecture of the shells,
The hollow sculpture of the fires,
Where memory, to grope its way,
Must seek in absence and dismay
The landmarks that it most admires.

But ages to this blackened tower
Will harness their momentous race
To find, like Tagus at its base,
A station of electric power
Whose Dynamo and sleepless mill
The Christian world with light may fill
And grind its life-sustaining flour:

Where faith-starved multitudes may quarry
As in a mountain, and be fed.
And well might Hell feel sick and sorry
To see the brown monks lying dead,
Where, as with coarse tarpaulins spread,
Each seemed a fifty-horsepower lorry
That to the troops had brought the Bread!

Their wounds were swords – how bravely worth
The care the angels took to smith them!
We thought they took their victory with them
But they had brought it down to earth,
For it was from their neighbouring spire
The proud Alcazar[64] caught the fire
Which gave that splendour phoenix-birth.

---

[64] From 20 July to 27 September 1936, the Nationalists under Colonel Moscardó were besieged in the fortress of the Alcazar in Toledo. The besiegers tried to set fire to the fortress and made several unsuccessful attempts to blow it up. The siege was finally lifted by the advancing Nationalist armies. See "The Alcazar Mined."

A phoenix from its ash to father,
A greater, in its turn, to sire –
It was to be to the Alcazar
What the Alcazar is to Spain,
And Spain is to the world entire;
Unanimous in blood and fire
A single purpose lit the twain!

La Mancha in Wartime[65]

A land of crosses, in the law's despite,
Where every chance designs a crucifix,
For the cicadas, in their choir of sticks
And for the wider, in the kestrel's flight.
The kestrel, and the stationary mill
That sail-less hangs upon the tide of war,
Had not this one significance before
With which their merest shadow signs the hill.
Where men have waifed the land with fire and steel
Of all it spreads its arms to represent,
Amidst their huge abortion of intent,
That symbol is the only thing that's real.
Where widowed of its sign, all they possessed,
The lonely hamlets semaphore their loss,
As in this next, where, half the waste across
Three giant windmills[66] crucify the West,
Each mule-slow road, beneath a plangent sky
Pursues its destination like a ghost,
A Station of the Cross at every post

---

[65] Town in Spain. Don Quixote, the eponymous hero of Miguel de Cervantes's novel (1605). Campbell identified himself with this figure.
[66] Don Quixote tilted at windmills, i.e. he undertook impossible and meaningless tasks.

In silent repetition filing by
While to each gust, as to an angry blow,
From post to post through leagues of groaning wire,
The tons of metal sound their mournful lyre
Vibrating to a thunderstorm of woe.
The Earth, that patient labourer for blows,
It seems, that brays prophetic from the metal,
Defrauded of the life-sufficing nettle
For promises of corn that never grows:
From whose whacked sides, that can support no more,
Its Maker to the madness cries a halt
Reclaiming from each desecrated vault
The sign that only martyrs can restore;
For in these paths blind pilgrims seem to flee,
And every road's a search to find the Cross,
By nothing more assented than its loss
That towers like midnight and outroars the sea.

Mary after the Red Terror[67]

When the anopheles were blithe
And life with fever played the whore:
And Death was plying at his scythe
Like a great oarsman at his oar:

And all along that fearful trip
That scorned the vengeance of the past,
I saw the world, a sinking ship,
As from the summit of its mast:

---

[67] The "Red Terror" was a period of chaos that engulfed Spain after the elections that brought a Socialist government to power in that country in February 1936, and which helped to precipitate the outbreak of the Civil War in July that year. Campbell and his family were living in Toledo during the period of the "Terror"; Campbell himself was badly beaten by the left-wing Assault Guards in March 1936, while Mary was many times threatened by left-wing *pistoleros* as she went to Mass. There were almost daily political murders in and around Toledo during this period.

Dingdonging in the lunar steeple
Of madness, with a wound to nurse,
For food and drink I asked the people
But all they gave me was a curse:

Then when we strays were roped and branded
(A burning cross upon the breast)
And in the old Corral were landed
Survivors of the rinderpest, –

You led me to the feet of Christ
Who threatened me with lifted quirt:
But by its loving fury sliced
I staggered upright from the dirt:

And that is why I do not simper,
Nor sigh, nor whine in my harangue.
Instead of ending with a whimper,
My life will finish with a bang!

"Poems for Spain"[68]

No sooner had its sales begun
Than all the reds were on the run
And only halted (sink or swim!)
To hack each other limb from limb –
So, once, at least beneath the sun
Poetic Justice has been done!

---

[68] The title is that of an anthology of left-wing poets published shortly before Franco's final victories ended the Civil War.

From *Flowering Rifle*

And, since the pain and sorrow of the world
Was far too soft a pillow, fiercely hurled
Their empire to the ends of the Abyss,
Searching the gulfs of the subconscious mind
New fiends to conquer, continents to find,
And ray their thoughts like comets to the blind:
Who face to face would meet with fiery beams
The eyeless monsters that molest our dreams
To show the way they can be faced and routed –
And Freud[69], the pervert's Bible, gaily flouted.
And his worst nightmares they had foxed from earth
And hunted down – an age before his birth,
When the subhuman dream, to its derision,
Confronted by the clear seraphic vision,
Shrunk like a squid: and left the wakened sprite
To sun its clouds with valour and delight –
All our psychology so damp and dreary,
By practice mastered, where we grope with theory,
By conquest answered, where we pose the query –
Where ours leave off by darkness circled in,
Their terrible discoveries begin,
And far across the line where we draw rein
Their fiery beacons light the fearful plain,
Over the wreck of battles fiercely won,
The vanguard and the outposts of the Sun!
Was this the race that could be tamely fed
On the Utopian blarney of the Red,
Or bribed to trade its devil-daring breath
For slavery, equality, and death:

---

[69] Sigmund Freud (1856-1939), Jewish Austrian founder of psychoanalysis and father figure of modern psychiatry. Enormously influential until quite recently – especially in artistic circles, but also generally among the western bourgeoisie – his activities extended beyond the treatment of neuroses to an assertively atheistic interpretation of a human nature rooted in thwarted incestuous desire and cryptic sex or death urges.

And, if these lying promises were truth,
For cheaper bread renounce its flaming youth –
Or the religion of the heart and head
For that of the soft belly and its bread? ...

It's better to bow down to wood and stone
And worship them with human sacrifice
Than worship nothing at this bloodier price
Of millions slain for greater filth and famine;
Since every "Reformation" we examine
That sprung from lack of Christian Resignation
Has plunged the world in deeper desolation:
And "Progress" is another way of trying
To kill an invalid, to stop him dying,
To rid the world of pain on the assumption
That colds are cured by Galloping Consumption.
The Inquisition in six hundred years
Pumped not a thousandth of the blood and tears
As, in some twenty, has the world-reforming,
Free-thinking, Rational, Cathedral-storming
Humanitarian, with his brother love,
To whom Tsarism was a sucking dove
And Hitler was to this degrading sham,
As to a rabid skunk, a snow-white lamb.
The pains of godless scientists[70] and scholars
Have brought us worse than Patagonian squalors,[71]
Saharan Famine, Dust-bowls, creeping drought,
Death in the Spirit and despair without,
And yet today the thinkers and the sages
Can patronize the towering middle ages
As being somewhat Bigoted and Narrow –
The sow of Bigotry could never farrow
Until the true freethinker came along

---

[70] "This was written before Einstein made us a present of the atom bomb." – Campbell's note.
[71] In *On the Origin of Species by Natural Selection*, Darwin describes the Patagonians as being very dirty people.

And liberated "Reason" grew so strong,[72]
Intolerance into delirium blazing
And Bigotry the hair of crime upraising –
To justify whatever Inquisition
To such a lust of blood could be physician,
Restoring it to its intended place
As warder and protector of the Race –
They made mere lunacy limp far behind,
And all the bloodiest manias of the mind,
To this of souls, seem innocent and kind:
Till one could wish a death by their own knout
To those who made religions out of doubt
Like rabid bloodhounds maddening men to slaughter
Who blame their hydrophobia on the Water:
Which by its raving could convince a clod
Of the reality and life of God
Whose absence roared so terribly, Whose lack
Could so disfigure, mutilate and hack
(Worse than their victims) those whom it afflicted,
Who seemed, from human lineaments evicted,
To roar and whinny like the ghouls of Hell
Which (if not elsewhere) here was proved as well,
Converting me to seek Him on the spot,
To see that foul Abyss where He was not:
To find no evidence my sense to dim
But to pure Evil was the lack of Him,
Exasperated to a white-hot glow
By the mere consciousness that this was so –
As it proclaimed itself in speech and fact
And by the loathing in each studied act.
And this identity alone sufficed
To drive an open reason straight to Christ...

---

[72] "More people have been imprisoned for Liberty, humiliated and tortured for Equality, and slaughtered for Fraternity, in this century than, for any less hypocritical motives, during the whole of the Middle Ages." – Campbell's note. For recent confirmation of this, see *The Black Book of Communism*, Harvard University Press.

But where the more celestial gardens grow
Beyond the crystal chandeliers of snow,
Thorning his breast upon a tusk of ice,
A nightingale in rapture, breathing spice,
A swan in hue, expiring as he sings,
A phoenix in the fulgence of his wings,
The Sun himself consumes a richer pyre
With clouds for cinders, bleeding scented fire,
And pours the ashes of his flowery slaughter
To foam in gold along the rose-red water,
Wherein the Eagle City steeps her towers
Besieged by the aroma of her flowers,
While, like Veronica,[73] the Tagus[74] sweeps,
And on her flood the dear reflection keeps.
There mirrored in the water upside down,
She laves the poison'd spittle from her crown
Which Jews and Saxons[75] squirt in Parthian flight
From inky glands, the loligos[76] of spite –
With ruins in the freshening water sunk
To cleanse the tail-shot of the human skunk,
For Hell itself the deed with dirt must sign
To prove her queenly titles are divine;
And hers to none in history shall yield,
Where Christ the sword, and Mary was the shield,–
Lepanto,[77] or the Catalaunian Field![78]

---

[73] Saint Veronica's napkin, with which Christ wiped his brow while carrying the cross on the way to the crucifixion, miraculously retained an image of his face.
[74] A River that flows around Toledo.
[75] A reference to what Campbell felt to be the consistently anti-Catholic reporting of the Civil War on the part of English and Jewish journalists at the time. With the outbreak of World War II, Campbell, who was opposed to the Nazis from the beginning, began to feel awkward about these and other distasteful remarks he had made about the Jews; and this change of heart can be seen in the rather defensive remarks of later poems such as "The Hoopoe." This is an example of the way in which Campbell often shoots himself in the foot by allowing his vitriol to get the better of him. For more on this, see Joseph Pearce, *Bloomsbury and Beyond: The Friends and Enemies of Roy Campbell*, Harper Collins, 2001.
[76] A loligo is a sort of squid.

For here the Tartar's dreams were put to flight,
And Europe rescued in her own despite.
  With turrets turned to deep artesian wells
Where submarine cathedrals ring their bells,
A lotus in each loophole seems to flower
Where late the maxim hailed its deadly shower,
While irises in every crater show
And stars replace them when they cease to glow.
She seems with blooms and perfumes to rehearse
The Saga she commanded from my verse.
For see the lilies that for flames aspire
To take her ramparts with redeeming fire,
With spring to capture, and with buds reclaim
What Earthquake, Fire, or Thunder could not tame,
Vulcan beneath, or Jupiter above –
Capitulating to the touch of Love!
Down the grey gorge, the Tagus, burning red,
Circles the Eagle City with its fire.
The Requetés[79] their rosary have said:
The Angelus rings out from every spire:
And from its height, among its sister-cones
The mountain with its garrison of stones,
With husky echo carries on the choir.
The Virgin of the Valley watched the town
Above the headlong river looking down,

---

[77] Famous naval battle fought on 7 October 1571, in which the European allies crushed a much greater Turkish force at Lepanto in the Gulf of Corinth. This proved to be the final blow to Muslim sea power.

[78] One of the first places in Spain to be colonized by the Romans. It was overrun by the Goths in the fifth century and was later the scene of battles between the Moors and the Christians in which the former were defeated. More recently it has been a restless part of Spain, involved in Carlist and other troubles.

[79] "The Scarlet Berets of the Requetés – chiefly Basques – The famous Carlist militia which saved Spain at the beginning of the Civil War, when the army was disarmed and disorganized. And the Red Terror was loosed on the defenceless populace. These civilians at the battle of Oriamindi, in the last century, although without artillery, defeated a British Regular Army under Gen. Sir Lacy Evans." – Campbell's note.

Upon whose flood reflected angels soar
In flames of blood to skim the liquid ore,
Where swallows must descend to kiss those skies
To which their matchless wings can never rise
Except by stooping downwards to adore.

From *A Letter from the San Mateo Front*

Storks to the steeples, rollers to the wires
Return, and swallows to the broken spires –
And men to the religion of their Sires!
Over the blood of martyrs scarcely dry
Toledo, there, against the morning sky
Like some great battle-cruiser from the fight
Returned with Victory (terrific sight!).
God's flagship, she, with shattered sides, presents
Her leaning funnels and her gaping rents,
In high salute uplifts her steepled guns,
And far the deep reverberation runs –
Through echoing gorges of the hills it roars
The listening plain receives it and adores
And at her mast the Royal Ensign soars,
Where one ecstatic eagle soars and faints,
And morning like a red and golden banner
Is roaring in the hurricane hosanna
Of the Heroes, and the Martyrs, and the Saints!

The Prodigal

John Bull, go fatten up your Son
Against my passing by,
And Jackie Calf! be underdone
Whether you roast or fry;
I'll take my time of Day from none –
Go carefully, say I!

When clocks like whirling windmills turn
And scarcely pause to chime
Like fast propellers at the stern
Of disappearing Time,
Then Time's to squander, Time's to burn,
And Leisure is no crime.

You've slung the World upon a cord
Your pendulum of rock;
Its every beat though you record,
I care no tick nor tock –
The Pen is mightier than the Sword,
But slower than the Clock.

Amphitryon[80] may toot his horn
And puff-puff run to date,
But leisure was my cash and corn
Who've loitered in my gait,
Nor died of hurry, nor was born
Through fear of being late.

---

[80] Mythological Greek king – huntsman, warrior, cuckold and stepfather of Hercules – who achieved his goals by cunning. He is the subject of plays by Plautus, Dryden, Molière, Giraudoux, and Camões, the great Portuguese poet Campbell admired and translated.

The Hoopoe[81]

Amongst the crags of thyme and samphire,[82]
The wastes of rosemary and fennel,
Up where the wolves in safety kennel
And by the gypsies' lonely campfire,
And round Toledo's shattered walls,
Where, like a crater in the moon,
The desecrated grandeur sprawls –
Though out of season, pitch, and tune,
All day the boding hoopoe calls.

The fire-bird flits amongst the cattle,
Pronouncing victory or doom,
The flashing corposant of battle,
The torch upon the hero's tomb,
The feathered tomahawk that waves
The bonnet of the redskin braves,
And cries once more his warning cry,
Before the grass has healed the graves
Or yet our open wounds be dry.

The comet of approaching war,
He flashes singing through the land,
And where his fiery crest is fanned
The farmyard poultry cluck no more.
Do cage-bred fowls resent this ranger
Of climes, who is the friend of danger
Yet visits, too, their sunless sky?
Is he not, too, a Southern Stranger
Whose gestures they would modify? –

---

[81] Spanish peasants regarded the hoopoe as a bird of ill-omen. Campbell here treats it as a friendly conveyor of warning.
[82] Cliff plant with aromatic saline fleshy leaves used in pickles (from the French, *herbe de Saint Pierre*).

But who has modified their own!
To have the lowdown from their cross-Fates,
Predicting tons of human phosphates
Imported here in flesh and bone,
When fiercely hooting on my Klaxon,[83]
Before our impetus was known,
I prophesied to Jew and Saxon
The flower-bed they would lay their backs on,
To fodder for our horses grown!

Did I conceal the yawn of loss
They crazed their Gadarene[84] to fly at —
Their Chaos by our solar Fiat,
Their Red Hell foundered by the Cross? —
When long before the bird was singing,
My cattle-whoop and whip were ringing
To head them, if I could, from harm,
Who to our knees for mercy clinging
Would have us exorcize the charm.

So, when the crazed herds rush the canyon,
Converging to the fearful jam,
One rider, their sole sane companion
May race his warning shots to slam,
Desisting as their spate grows thicker
While lifted tails revolve and flicker
Like froth-suds on their frenzied flood,
Till ribs and horns, like crumpled wicker,
And beeves are crushed, like grapes of blood.

---

[83] Klaxon: a powerful electric motor-horn. In the Introduction to *Flowering Rifle*, Campbell claimed to have predicted the outbreak and the outcome of the Spanish Civil War in such poems as "The Fight", written before 1936.
[84] Reference to the drowning of the Gadarene swine (Mark 5:1) into whose bodies the demons exorcised by Christ fled for refuge.

Are these the thanks their friends have shown us –
To have me outlawed, gagged, and tied?[85] –
When shouldering a thankless onus,
I blazed the warning far and wide,
Deserving, rather, of a bonus
For vigilance, than bards who lied,
For butchers' bribes, to foolish readers,
And were the rustlers, and stampeders,
And contrabanders in their hide.

With cheap Utopian bait a fisher,
A Market-Angler with the Pen,
Did I ensnare the raw militia
Before they had the sense of men?
Was I the one to bomb their hearse
With saurian millstones, tear by tear,
And then anthologize their verse
To feed the huge wolf-bellied purse
He hugged, so safely, in the rear?

Did I the good cabestro[86] sham,
A King's gold medal round my neck,
Like some sleek bell-decoying ram,
To clank my bookfans to their wreck?
Did I in Mayfair[87] have my fling
And traffic in the slaughtered youth
Who might have lived to serve their King?
Or was I there to prove my truth,
(I think so!) where the bullets sing?

---

[85] A reference to the literary boycott from which Campbell suffered in the years before WWII.
[86] Domestic ox (Spanish). The cabestro is used to lead bulls into the arena – hence, a treacherous decoy.
[87] Fashionable London district.

I like this Sergeant of the Birds
With three white chevrons on his wings.
He knows that deeds say more than words
But on the battlefield he sings –
While birds who fatten on the dead
And farm the carnage from behind
For gold or offal – cower in dread:
Poets, the vultures of the mind,
And those by nature born and bred.

For when the War-Cloud forks their sky,
They'll seek Utopias overseas
To jobs in ministries they'll fly,
And funk-holes in the BBC[88]
Where, snugly pocketing the kitty,
They'll sell their pale commercial pity,
In posh editions, for us mere
Shock-workers of the Camp and City
Whose sweat, and life-blood, is their beer.

Before me as the hoopoe cries,
I see a fiercer flag unrolled
Eclipsing now the red and gold
Infanta[89] of the evening skies.
For now all other flags turn black
Save there, against the stormy rack,
Three crosses in a single wheel
The spectrum of the light they lack,
And rainbow of the showers of steel!

---

[88] A reference to Stephen Spender (1909-1995), poet, literary critic and editor of *Horizon* (1939-1941) and *Encounter* (1953-1967). Together with his friends, the poets W.H. Auden (1907-1973), Louis MacNiece (1907-1963), Cecil Day-Lewis (1904-1972), and novelist Christopher Isherwood (1906-1986), he was at the heart of the left-wing literary movement of the 1930s. Campbell lampooned the first four of them as MacSpaunday. They had all modified or abandoned their radicalism by the 1950s.

[89] Infanta: daughter of the King and Queen of Spain. The Spanish flag consists of red and gold horizontal stripes.

But this no miracle-crusade
Won in our hearts before we strike;
Rather a punishment-parade
For friend and enemy alike;
Yet when the mealy mouths are heard
Of those who prostitute the word
And in the rearguard pimp for hire,
It's time to imitate the bird
Who preens his chevrons under fire!

To hear the Fire-bird change his score
And match his war-whoop to the drum
As scarce in twenty years before –
"Big Medicine" it was for some
Who with the hoopoe scoop the news
That is not printed in reviews –
The kind they stoned the prophets for,
And lumbering progress never views
Except to boycott or ignore.

This Bird be my heraldic crest
Because his prophecies are banned:
He chucks a regimental chest
And flits across the burning sand
To share those gifts of high bestowal
That seraphim bequeathed our sires
One winter night broadcasting "Noel!"
(Strange news for Isidore and Joel)[90]
To cattlemen by wayside fires.

Was that reported in "The Prattler"[91]
Or "The New Yes-man"[92] of those times,
Or like a diamond-headed rattler

---

[90] i.e. Jews.
[91] *The Tatler*, a London journal.
[92] A reference to the *New Statesman*, a London journal with left-wing sympathies.

Suppressed, along with Herod's crimes,
While he monopolized the Glaxo[93]
And sopped his bib with granny's tears –
Though in a record flood for years
The baby-killing he attacks so
Had soaked him crimson to the ears![94]

To cock the wind this flame-red feather,
In my sombrero, be the sign
Prophetic of the coming weather
With no false hankering to "fine",
And the diploma of a knowledge
So far beyond the scope of college
That whatsoever catch we croon,
Ages and continents, to acknowledge,
In blood or lava scrawl the rune.

The Clock in Spain[95]

This Clock from England says he came
Where as a God he was revered.
His hours in length were all the same,
And each departed whence it came
The moment its relief appeared.

To a great Firm his line he traces,
Of manufacturers the aces,
And if you don't believe it's true,
The legend written on his face is
"Birmingham 1922".

---

[93] Glaxo-Allenbury's, a British company, and manufacturers of baby products: hence Glaxo, any sop to soothe an infant.
[94] Campbell believed that the British press had deliberately suppressed accounts of massacres of Christians by the Spanish Socialist forces.
[95] Inspired by an old clock Campbell and his wife had bought, inscribed "Birmingham 1922", the place and date of their wedding.

Squire[96] was the Auden[97] of those days
And Shanks[98] the Spender[99] of our trade;
For there the Clock awards the bays
And tells the prophets when to fade
Or die of one another's praise.

Like a policeman on his beat
The despot ticked with measured tread,
Dictating when to sleep, or eat,
Or drink – for in the darkest street
No Pub could open till he said.

Hours never telescoped in one
Disjointed by the lovers' thrill,
Nor made the night like water run
To strand the flushed and gasping sun,
Dumbfounded, on their windowsill.

Big Ben proclaimed, through mists of grime,
The surly fascism of Time,
And all the small Benitos,[100] then,
Would cuckoo, tinkle, chirp, or chime
Their orders to the race of men.

Some Red Brigader, panic-shod,
Abandoned here, on Spanish sod,
This sacred fetish of his race
He'd fought to substitute for God –

---

[96] Sir John Squire (1884-1958), editor of the *London Mercury*, critic, gifted parodist, and minor Georgian poet.
[97] W.H. Auden (1907-1973), important poet and translator; also dramatist and critic. The most prominent of the left-wing poets of the 1930s, he later became more conservative and a fairly devout Anglican under the influence of C.S. Lewis, Charles Williams and Kierkegaard.
[98] Edward Shanks was a close associate of Squire's on the *London Mercury*.
[99] Stephen Spender.
[100] Benito Mussolini (1883-1945), Italian Fascist dictator.

So we took pity on his case:

And placed him on the mantel here,
Where still he ticked with might and main,
Though, like his countrymen, in vain,
With local ways to interfere
And stop the history of Spain.

The Sun would pause to hear a song
And loiter, when he chose to chime,
Which always put him in the wrong:
And folk would dance the whole night long
When he proclaimed it closing time.

His heart was broken by the trains
Which left him panting hours ahead:
And he was liable to sprains,
For on the wall we knocked his brains
Each time he shrilled us out of bed.

Like Bonaparte upon his isle
Confronted by Sir Hudson Lowe,[101]
The Despot lost his haughty style
Recalling with a rueful dial
His pomp and pride of long ago.

But when, athwart an open door,
He smelt the orange-trees in flower
And heard the headlong Tagus roar,
And saw the white sierras[102] soar,
That moment cost him half an hour.

---

[101] Sir Hudson Lowe (1769-1844), English general during the Napoleonic wars. Governor of Saint Helena during Napoleon's exile there.
[102] Sierra: long, jagged mountain-chain.

And when amidst the poplars white
He heard the nightingales unite
To drown the torrent's hoarse furore,
And held his breath from sheer delight –
It lost him fifty minutes more!

About the time of our Fiesta,
When gales from the meseta[103] sweep
To strew the roses fetlock-deep –
He fell into his first siesta,
And now he often has a sleep.

But what served most to change his story
And turn his notions outside in –
This clock so querulous and hoary
Beheld my love, in all her glory,
Clearing for action to the skin:

Her hair that smokes with raven swirl
To tell of banked and hidden fire,
And golden dynamos that whirl
To launch a battleship of pearl
Into the rollers of desire.

He saw her deep dark eyes ignite
Like radium, or the northern light
That through the blackening ether flies,
And to the voltage of delight
In glittering swordplay fall and rise.

Her eyelashes with jet-black sting
Like scorpions curved: and dark as night
The chevrons on her brows that spring
Like feathers in a condor's wing
Arching their splendour in the height:

---

[103] Plateau (Spanish).

The ivory, the jet, the coral,
The dainty groove that dints her back
To take the sting from every moral
And make each jealousy or quarrel
The fiercer aphrodisiac.

The lips that burn, like crimson chillies:
The valleys where the thyme uncloses:
The haunches like a bounding filly's:
Her breasts like bruised and bouncing roses –
And all the rest a field of lilies!

The room revolving like a wheel,
The romp, the tussle, then the fight,
The croup of galloping delight
Where rapture rides with rowelled[104] heel,
Without a bridle, through the night.

Since then our clock has ceased to rail
Or tick the time, as if he knew
Time cannot change or custom stale
Those roses roaring in the gale
That, as I rode, around me blew.

Today more tractable you'll find him
And less on edge than was his wont.
In sprays of lilac we've enshrined him:
He stops the moment that you wind him,
Then starts up ticking, if you don't.

And now the pastures breathe their spice,
Twinkling with thyme and fresh anemone,
That punctuality's a vice
He swears today – and what a price
To have to pay for world-hegemony!

---

[104] The rowel is the spiked revolving disc at the end of a spur.

So silent with his rusty bell,
This ancient veteran of the shelf,
Whom I can neither pawn nor sell,
Reminds me somewhat of myself,
And if you want the reason, well,

Although he may appear to you
To have renounced his race and era,
His steel is British, cold, and blue,
As ever flashed at Waterloo
Or held the line at Talavera.[105]

And if the dreadful hour should chime
For British blood, find steel as grim,
My clock will wake, and tick the time,
And slope his arms and march – and I'm
The one to fall in step with him.

The loud fire-eating propheteers
Will cross the drink in craven fears,
Or worse, like vulture, crow, and kite-hawk,
Engage in money-making fight-talk
And pick the bones of fusiliers.

Coining the opulence of Babbitts,[106]
Out of the cowardice of rabbits
And mealy kisses of Iscariot,
More plutocratic in their habits,
The more they woo the proletariat –

---

[105] Spanish town, the site of a battle during the Peninsular wars in which Wellington defeated Napoleon's troops in 1809.
[106] A reference to the leading character in Sinclair Lewis's novel, *Babbitt* (1922). Typifies the businessman of orthodox outlook and virtues, with no interest in cultural values.

In vain you'll ask of them the hour
When zero has begun to chime,
And that which pushed this idle pen
Will strike it forth in bursts that rhyme,
The trigger-finger on the Bren.[107]

One Transport Lost[108]

Where, packed as tight as space can fit them
The soldiers retch, and snore, and stink,
It was no bunch of flowers that hit them
And woke them up, that night, to drink.

Dashing the bulkheads red with slaughter,
In the steep wash that swept the hold,
Men, corpses, kitbags, blood, and water,
Colliding and commingling rolled.

Some clung, like flies, in fear and wonder,
Clutched to the crossbeams, out of reach,
Till sprayed from thence by jets of thunder
That spouted rumbling from the breach.

In this new world of blast and suction,
The bulkhead tilted to a roof;
Friend aided friend – but to destruction,
And valour seemed its own reproof.

---

[107] British light machine-gun.
[108] Written in February 1943. The troop-ship in which Campbell was travelling to East Africa ran into engine trouble off the Irish coast where it floundered for five days. This poem deals with the incident.

Forced by the pent explosive airs
In the huge death-gasp of its shell,
Or sucked, like Jonah,[109] by their prayers
From forth that spiracle[110] of Hell –

The ones that catapulted from it
Saw the whole hull reverse its dome,
Then ram the depths, like some huge comet,
Flood-lit with phosphorus and foam.

The shark and grampus might reprieve,
After their jaunt upon a raft,
The few that got Survivors' Leave –
But those who perished would have laughed!

Their fiercest thirst they've quenched and cupped,
And smashed the glass (this life of slaves!);
No hectoring Redcaps[111] interrupt
Their fornication with the waves.

For us, this world of Joad[112] and Julian,[113]
The dithering of abortive schemes;
For them, the infinite, cerulean
Suspension of desires and dreams.

So save your Bait, you Bards and Thinkers!
For us who daren't refuse to chew
Hook, line, and swivel, trace and sinkers,
And rod and all, and like it too!

---

[109] The Old Testament prophet who spent three days in the belly of a great fish or whale.
[110] Spiracle: blow-hole of whales.
[111] Military policemen, so called because of the red band they wear round their caps.
[112] Professor C.E.M. Joad (1891-1953), British author specializing in popularized philosophy. Broadcaster during World War II and member of The Brains Trust. He converted from atheism to Anglicanism at the end of his life. Campbell disliked him for his pacifism and his left-wing political views.
[113] Sir Julian Huxley (1887-1975), British biologist and apologist for "religion without revelation". Brother of Aldous Huxley.

For them, the wave, the melancholy
Chant of the wind that tells no lies;
The breakers roll their funeral volley
To which the thundering cliff replies.

The black cape-hens in decent crêpe
Will mourn them till the Last Event;
The roaring headlands of the Cape
Are lions on their monument.

Luis de Camões[114]

Camões, alone, of all the lyric race,
Born in the black aurora of disaster,
Can look a common soldier in the face:
I find a comrade where I sought a master:
For daily, while the stinking crocodiles
Glide from the mangroves on the swampy shore,
He shares my awning on the dhow,[115] he smiles,
And tells me that he, lived it all before.
Through fire and shipwreck, pestilence and loss,
Led by the *ignis fatuus*[116] of duty
To a dog's death – yet of his sorrows king –
He shouldered high his voluntary Cross,
Wrestled his hardships into forms of beauty,
And taught his gorgon[117] destinies to sing.

---

[114] Luis de Camões (1524-1580), Portugal's greatest poet, one of the great poets of European literature. His epic, *The Lusiads*, was written while serving as a soldier during voyages to India during which he suffered many disasters. Campbell wrote of Camões: "[he] is the soldier's poet par excellence... I wrote the... sonnet to express the real comradeship he finally inspires."
[115] "Lateen-rigged Arab, Persian or Indian sailing craft." – Campbell's note.
[116] Will o' the wisp.

ROY CAMPBELL

Imitation (and Endorsement) of the Famous Sonnet of Bocage Which He Wrote on Active Service Out East

Camões, great Camões! though twins in form
Tally the cursed fates that love to plague us,
Exchanging for our vineyards by the Tagus
The Sacrilegious Headland[118] and the Storm:
Though, like yourself, from Chindwin to Zambezi[119]
In wars and fearful penury I wander,
On vain desires my fevered sighs to squander,
And on the thorns of memory sleep uneasy:
Though trampled by the same vindictive doom,
I pray for sudden death to come tomorrow
And know that peace lies only in the tomb:
And though in shame and all precarious shifts
You were my model – mine's the crowning sorrow
To share your luck, but lack your towering gifts.

Dreaming Spires[120]

Through villages of yelping tykes[121]
With skulls on totem-poles, and wogs[122]
Exclaiming at our motor bikes
With more amazement than their dogs:

---

[117] (Or Medusa): snake-haired monster of Greek mythology whose glance turned men to stone. Slain by the hero Perseus.
[118] "Sacrilegious Headland: The Cape of Good Hope, the spirit of which is personified by Camões in *The Lusiads* as the blasphemous giant, Adamastor." – Campbell's note.
[119] Great rivers; the Chindwin in upper Burma, and the Zambesi, which forms the boundary between Zimbabwe and Zambia.
[120] Written in hospital in Mombassa in March 1944. Campbell had been in the observation unit of the force training under Wingate on motorcycles at the foot of Mount Kilimanjaro. He had travelled through the Athi Game Park.
[121] Dogs (slang).
[122] Blacks (slang).

Respiring fumes of pure phlogiston[123]
On hardware broncos, half-machine,
With arteries pulsing to the piston
And hearts inducting gasoline:

Buckjumping over ruts and boulders,
The Centaurs of an age of steel
Engrafted all save head and shoulders
Into the horsepower of the wheel –

We roared into the open country,
Scattering vultures, kites, and crows;
All Nature scolding our effrontery
In raucous agitation rose.

Zoology went raving stark
To meet us on the open track –
The whole riff raff of Noah's Ark
With which the wilderness was black.

With kicks and whinnies, bucks and snorts,
Their circuses stamped by:
A herd of wildebeest cavorts,
And somersaults against the sky:

Across the stripes of zebras sailing,
The eyesight rattles like a cane
That's rattled down an area-railing
Until it blurs upon the brain.

The lions flee with standing hackles,
Leaving their feast before they've dined:
Their funeral poultry flaps and cackles
To share the breeze they feel behind.

---

[123] Principle of inflammability formerly supposed to exist in combustible bodies.

Both wart- and road-hog vie together,
As they and we, petarding[124] smoke,
Belly to earth and hell for leather,
In fumes of dust and petrol choke.

We catch the madness they have caught,
Stand on the footrests, and guffaw –
Til shadowed by a looming thought
And visited with sudden awe,

We close our throttles, clench the curb,
And hush the rumble of our tyres,
Abashed and fearful to disturb
The City of the Dreaming Spires[125] –

The City of Giraffes! – a People
Who live between the earth and skies,
Each in his lone religious steeple,
Keeping a light-house with his eyes:

Each his own stairway, tower, and stylite,[126]
Ascending on his saintly way
Up rungs of gold into the twilight
And leafy ladders to the day:

Chimneys of silence! at whose summit,
Like storks, the daydreams love to nest;
The Earth, descending like a plummet
Into the oceans of unrest,

---

[124] Petard: Small engine of war formerly used to blow in door etc.; a kind of firework.
[125] Oxford is known as the city of the dreaming spires.
[126] A pillar. Saint Simeon and some other eastern saints between the fourth and tenth centuries lived on pillars (often not more than a few feet high) as a form of mortification to balance the extreme sensuality of the people among whom they lived.

They can ignore – whose nearer neighbour
The sun is, with the stars and moon
That on their hides, with learned labour,
Tattooed the hieroglyphic rune.

Muezzins[127] that from airy pylons
Peer out above the golden trees
Where the mimosas[128] fleece the silence
Or slumber on the drone of bees:

Nought of this earth they see but flowers
Quilting a carpet to the sky
To where some pensive crony towers
Or Kilimanjaro takes the eye.

Their baser passions fast on greens
Where, never to intrude or push,
Their bodies live like submarines,
Far down beneath them, in the bush.

Around their head the solar glories,
With their terrestrial sisters fly –
Rollers,[129] and orioles,[130] and lories,[131]
And trogons[132] of the evening sky.

Their bloodstream with a yeasty leaven
Exalts them to the stars above,
As we are raised, though not to heaven,
By drink – or when we fall in love.

---

[127] Muslim crier who proclaims the hours of prayer from a minaret.
[128] A kind of leguminous shrub.
[129] Brilliant-plumaged bird related to the crow.
[130] Bird with black and golden plumage.
[131] Bright-plumaged parrot-like bird.
[132] Sleek, gorgeous, long-tailed bird.

By many a dismal crash and wreck
Our dreams are weaned of aviation,
But these have beaten (by a neck!)
The steepest laws of gravitation.

Some animals have all the luck,
Who hurl their breed in nature's throat –
Out of a gumtree by a buck,
Or escalator – by a goat!

When I have worked my ticket, pension,
And whatsoever I can bum,
To colonize the fourth dimension,
With my Beloved, I may come,

And buy a pair of stilts for both,
And hire a periscope for two,
To vegetate in towering sloth
Out here amongst these chosen few...

Or so my fancies seemed to sing
To see, across the gulf of years,
The soldiers of a reigning King
Confront those ghostly halberdiers.

But someone kicks his starter back:
Anachronism cocks its ears.
Like Beefeaters who've got the sack
With their own heads upon their spears;

Like Leftwing Poets at the hint
Of Work, or danger, or the blitz,[133]
Or when they catch the deadly glint
Of satire, swordplay of the wits, –

---

[133] The bombing of London by the Germans in World War II.

Into the dusk of leafy oceans
They fade away with phantom tread;
And changing gears, reversing notions,
The road to Moshi[134] roars ahead.

The Skull in the Desert

(To Desmond MacCarthy[135])

I am not one his bread who peppers
With stars of nebulous illusion,
But learned, with soldiers, mules, and lepers
As comrades of my education,
The Economy of desolation
And Architecture of confusion

On the bare sands, where nothing else is
Save death, and like a lark in love,
Gyrating through the vault above,
The ace of all created things
Flies singing Gloria in Excelsis
And spreads the daybreak from his wings:

I found a horse's empty cranium,
Which the hyenas had despised,
Wherein the wind ventriloquized
And fluting huskily afar
Sang of the rose and geranium
And evenings lit with azahar.

---

[134] Town in Tanzania on the Kenyan border.
[135] Sir Desmond MacCarthy (1877-1952), editor of *Life and Letters*, one of the foremost literary critics of the period. One-time literary editor and dramatic critic of the *New Statesman*; later, on BBC's advisory committee, he arranged for Campbell to be employed there.

Foaled by the Apocalypse, and stranded
Some wars, or plagues, or famines back,
To bleach beside the desert track,
He kept his hospitable rule:
A pillow for the roving bandit,
A signpost to the stricken mule.

A willing host, adeptly able,
Smoking a long cheroot of flame,
To catalyse the sniper's aim
Or entertain the poet's dream,
By turns a gunrest or a table,
An inspiration, and a theme –

He served the desert for a Sphinx
And to the wind for a guitar,
For in the harmony he drinks
To rinse his whirring casque of bone
There hums a rhythm less its own
Than of the planet and the star.

No lion with a lady's face
Could better have become the spot
Interrogating time and space
And making light of their replies
As he endured the soldier's lot
Of dissolution, sand, and flies.

So white a cenotaph to show
You did not have to be a banker
Or poet of the breed we know:
Subjected to a sterner law,
The luckless laughter of the ranker[136]
Was sharked upon his lipless jaw.

---

[136] Private soldier (slang).

All round, the snarled and windrowed sands
Expressed the scandal of the waves,
And in this orphan of the graves
As in a conch, there seemed to roar
Reverberations of the Hand
That piles the wrecks along the shore.

Twice I had been the Ocean's refuse
As now the flotsam of the sand,
Far worse at sea upon the land
Than ever in the drink before
For Triton,[137] with his sons and nephews,
To gargle and to puke ashore.

To look on him, my tongue could taste
The bony mandibles of death
Between my cheeks: across the waste
The drought was glaring like a gorgon
But in that quaint outlandish organ
With spectral whinny, whirled the breath.

The wind arrived, the gorgon-slayer,
Defied the wind that rose to whelm it,
And swirled like water in the helmet
Of that dead brain, with crystal voices,
Articulating in a prayer
The love with which the rain rejoices –

The zephyr from the blue Nevadas,
Stirrupped with kestrels, smoothly rinking
The level wave where halcyons drowse,
Came with the whirr of the cicadas,
With the green song of orchards drinking
And orioles fluting in the boughs.

---

[137] Merman of Greek mythology.

All the green juices of creation,
And those with which our veins are red,
Were mingled in his jubilation
And sang the swansong of the planet
Amidst the solitudes of granite
And the grey sands that swathe the dead.

All I had left of will or mind,
Which fire or fever had not charred,
Was but the shaving, husk, and shard:
But that sufficed to catch the air
And from the Pentecostal wind
Conceive the whisper of a prayer.

And soon that prayer became a hymn
By feeding on itself. The skies
Were tracered by the seraphim
With arrows from the dim guitars
That on their strings funambulize[138]
The tap-dance of the morning stars.

When frowsy proverbs lose their force
And tears have dried their queasy springs,
To hope and pray for crowns and wings
It follows as a thing of course,
When you've phrenologized the horse
That on the desert laughs and sings.

I leave the Helmet and the Spear
To the hyena-bellied muses
That farm this carnage from the rear:
But of the sacrifice they fear
And of the strain their sloth refuses
Elect me as the engineer.

---

[138] To ropewalk.

Make of my bones your fife and organ,
Red winds of pestilence and fire!
But from the rust on the barbed-wire
And scurf upon the pool that stinks
I fetch a nosegay for the Gorgon
And a conundrum for the Sphinx:

For all the freight of Stygian[139] ferries,
Roll on the days of halcyon weather,[140]
The oriole fluting in the cherries,
The sunlight sleeping on the farms,
To say the Rosary together
And sleep in one another's arms!

The Beveridge Plan[141]

Through land and sea supreme
Without a rift or schism
Roll on the Wowser's[142] dream –
Fascidemokshevism!

Monologue

No disillusionment can gravel,
A mercenary volunteer
Who joins an alien force, to travel
And fight, for fifty pounds a year.

---

[139] The Styx was one of the nine rivers of Hades in Greek mythology; to cross the Styx in Charon's ferry was to die.
[140] The halcyon: a bird fabled by the ancients to breed in a floating nest on the sea at winter solstice, charming the wind and waves into calm for the purpose; hence, "halcyon days" – a period of calm. It is also the name of the Australian kingfisher.
[141] A reference to the Beveridge Report of 1942 that appeared in an English newspaper Campbell read on service in East Africa and which offered a picture of the future shape of British society.
[142] "Any kind of Puritan, killjoy, socialist and fabian, or pedant." – Campbell's note.

A grizzled sergeant of the pommies,[143]
A gaunt centurion of the wogs,
Can fall for no Utopian promise
The Bait of grasping demagogues.
Against the usurers of tears,
Fraternity, and all that dope,
I learned (while wet behind the ears)
The use of Nelson's telescope.[144]
The Left Wing Prophet, Bard, and Seer,
Sleek Babbitts of the Age to Be,
Who farm this carnage from the rear
Have yet to find a fly on me.
I know the love that shears our fleeces,
The love that makes our thinkers fools,
The love of thirty silver pieces –
A soldier's value, or a mule's!
The same for all who trade in doves
And fatten on the world's distress,
The pedlars of fraternal loves,
And creeping Shylocks[145] of the Press.
Against each rearguard propheteer
And Tartuffe[146] from the MOI,[147]
Experience wads my dainty ear,
And through the solemn bluff, my eye,
For bayonet-practice, punching sawdust,
Lets in the glint I love to see –
For where the sacking gapes the broadest
The daylight laughs and winks at me!

---

[143] The British (slang).
[144] At the Battle of Copenhagen in 1801, Admiral Hyde Parker, Nelson's first in command, hoisted a signal to break off the action. Putting his telescope to his blind eye, Nelson professed to see no signals and went on to win the battle.
[145] Colloquial term for a usurer. From the character of that name in Shakespeare's *The Merchant of Venice*.
[146] A hypocrite or religious hypocrite, from the character in Molière's play, *Le Tartuffe*.
[147] The Ministry of Information. Cecil Day-Lewis, poet, translator and left-wing associate of Auden and Spender (and later Poet Laureate) was editor of books and pamphlets for the MOI from 1941 to 1946.

I'm fighting for no better world
But for a worse – the blasted pit
Wherein the bones of this were hurled –
And our hegemony of it!
I'm fighting for a funkhole-warren
Of bureaucrats, who've come to stay,
Because I'd rather, than the foreign
Equivalent, it should be they.
We all become the thing we fight
Till differing solely in the palms
And fists that semaphore (to Right
Or Left) their imbecile salaams.[148]
Each of the other, fifty times,
Will plagiarize the stock-in-trade
Of purges, massacres, and crimes,
Before their hatred is allayed.
For I have lived, of three crusades,
The heroism and the pathos,
Seen how the daft illusion fades,
And learned of victory the bathos.
But when the lava has been poured
Through huge ravines of change and loss,
Of all most hated or adored,
One thing remains intact, the Cross!
It is the rifle on one's shoulder
That galls one on the endless march:
It is the backward-rolling boulder
We sisyphize[149] with backs that arch:
It is the axle of our lorry,
This breakdown planet, bogged in mire:
It is the road we stamp and quarry,
As prisoners, on the sands of fire:

---

[148] Salaam: oriental salutation "Peace."
[149] Reference to the Greek myth of Sisyphus, one of those tormented in Hades, having eternally to roll a rock up a hill from the top of which it always rolls down again.

It is the iron that brands us men –
Both friend and enemy as one,
The sword of Victory, and then
The Victor's crutch, when all is done!
Field Marshals, Captains, and Lieutenants
And we poor gunfood of the ranks,
Carry it as a curse or penance
Whether with blasphemy or thanks;
Whether rebelliously, or knowing
And prizing it for what it's worth –
All Heaven upon our thews bestowing
The Atlas-burden of the Earth.[150]

Let me be there to share the strain
And with the poorest pull my weight
As in the Catacombs of Spain
When all the world was Red with hate!
I know that all ideals miscarry,
That cowards use the blows we strike,
That liars aim the guns we carry
Screeching their hatred on the Mike.
Yet lest that burden touch the ground
I would be there to lift that prize,
And with the lowest conscript found
That ever "Freedom" chained with lies,
Rather than feast on poor men's bones
And cheat the worker of his bread
With Judas-kisses, sighs, and groans,
Between the armchair and the bed.
I love the hard and stony track
Where humour flashes from the flint,
And though on crutches crawling back
Trussed like a turkey on a splint –
If you should ask what other joy
Amongst my fellow-slaves I found:

---

[150] In Greek mythology, Atlas was a titan who supported the sky on his shoulders.

I date not speak, I am a Goy [151]–
One of the Christian Underground.
From there, whichever way they work us,
Will boomerang the last surprise –
Out of the red sands of the Circus
The great Cathedrals climbed the skies!

Auguries

Prepare for days of pallor,
Forget the waste of breath.
The day has died of valour,
The night will freeze to death.

And if tomorrow wake,
Comrades, no foe to bomb you,
All you had left to take
Will then be taken from you.

Your hunger, sold in books,
Will fetch huge dividends
To salary the cooks
Of other people's friends.

Your poverty, no more
Your own, but in their hands
Another sword of war
To desolate the lands –

What of yourselves you've wrested
From the devouring flames,
Commercialized, invested,
And harnessed to their aims.

---

[151] Gentile (Yiddish).

The selves you had, so brave
To suffer, help, and share,
Their pity will enslave
To ration with fresh air.

Their pale, commercial pity,
Conscripting thought and art,
That sits in hushed committee
To vivisect the heart.

The mealy mouth fraternal,
The opening of a purse
That sucks with greed eternal
The wounds it loves to nurse,

The Sucker (hear him smack it!)
Is hungry. Art and speech
Academize the racket
And laureate the leech.

I see the coming day
With golden gifts embrace
The lads who ran away
Or loitered at the base.

Now are the times when Fear
And Avarice grow fat
And drop a pitying tear
Into the pauper's hat.

What rankers paid in taxes
Will clink upon the bar
Where the Left Wing relaxes
In the Swiss or Bolivar.[152]

---

[152] Pubs in London.

But we with solemn faces
May hide a secret joy,
In subterranean places,
The laughter of the Goy,

To catacombs returning
Where faith and kindness hold.
And keep an altar burning
To other gods than Gold.

Reflections

While Echo[153] pined into a shade,
Narcissus, by the water's shelf,
Met with a lurking death, and made
An alligator of himself.

Of many selves we all possess
My meanest has the most persisted,
The one that joined the NFS[154]
When half humanity enlisted.

A shifty and insidious ghost,
Of all my selves he is the one,
Though it's with him I meet the most,
I'd go the longest way to shun.

---

[153] In Greek mythology, Narcissus was a beautiful youth who fell in love with his own reflection in a river. He pined away and died. In this he was being punished by the gods for his cruelty to Echo, a nymph who loved him and wooed him by repeating his words (her only form of speech). Having been repulsed, she wasted away with grief until nothing but her voice remained.

[154] The National Fire Service. This is a gratuitous gibe at Stephen Spender who joined the N.F.S. during the war. Campbell actually worked as an Air Raid Precautions warden for a short time before enlisting.

When manhood crests the full red stream
Of comradeship, and breasts the surge,
Dreaming a chilled, amphibious dream,
He haunts the shallows by the verge.

Out of the mirrors in hotels
He makes for me, but as I pass,
Recedes into their glazing wells
And leaves no ripples on the glass.

Along the windows of the shops,
And in the tankard's curving base,
I have surprised him as he drops
Into the void without a trace.

He shaves the surfaces: he snails
His sheeny track along the walls:
The windows seem a myriad scales
Through which an endless serpent crawls.

His form is one, his number legion:
He incubates in hushed platoons,
Denizens of the glassy region
And of the vitreous lagoons.

Each time I step into the street
I multiply his gliding swarms,
Along the panes to launch a fleet
Of bloodless and reptilian forms.

I know the scar upon his cheek,
His limp, his stare, his friendly smile –
Though human in his main physique,
Yet saurian in his lurking guile.

Well on this side of make-believe,
Though edging always to the flanks,

He wears my chevrons on his sleeve
As though he'd earned them in the ranks.

In him, behind each sheet of glaze,
A Eunuch with a bowstring hides:
Under each film, with lidless gaze,
A sleepless alligator slides.

Within his heart, so chilled and squamous,[155]
He knows I've but to sell my pride
To make him safe, and rich, and famous;
And he would fatten if I died.

In feigned petition from the sash
He swerves to me, and I from him:
But if one day you hear a splash,
You'll know he's fastened on a limb.

No ripple on the glassy frame
Will show you where a man was drowned;
But Echo, practising his Fame,
Will pine once more into a sound.

Washing Day

Amongst the rooftop chimneys where the breezes
Their dizzy choreography design,
Pyjamas, combinations, and chemises
Inflate themselves and dance upon the line.
Drilled by a loose disorder and abandon,
They belly and explode, revolve and swing,
As fearless of the precipice they stand on
As if there were religion in a string.

---

[155] Scale-like or scaly.

Annexing with their parachute invasion
The intimate behaviour of our life,
They argue, or embrace with kind persuasion,
And parody our dalliance or our strife.
We change ideas and moods like shirts or singlets,[156]
Which, having shed, they rise to mock us still:
And the wind laughs and shakes her golden ringlets
To set them independent of our will.
They curtsey and collapse, revolve and billow –
A warning that, when least aware we lie,
The dreams are incubated in our pillow
That animate its chrysalis to fly.

Rhapsody of the Man in Hospital Blues and the "Hyde Park Lancers"[157]

*(To the Memory of R.S.M. Charles Mulvey
of Princess Pat's Canadian Light Infantry)*

From Notting Hill to Prince's Gate[158]
I'd started breaking-in my stick
And of my new, three-legged gait
Acquired the quaint arithmetic.

No more to canter, trot or trippel,
Where dandies prance along the Row,
I coaxed the strange unwieldly cripple
I had become yet feared to know:

In spite of one so ill-adjusted,
So keenly to the task he warmed,
So eagerly to me he trusted,
So newly had he been deformed,

---

[156] Garment worn below shirt.
[157] The poem refers to Campbell's lameness.
[158] Notting Hill is a district to the northwest of Hyde Park and Kensington Gardens; Prince's Gate is at the southern end of the Gardens.

That though he seemed a drunken lout,
Less of a comrade than a weight,
I had no further choice or doubt
But to accept him as my fate.

(So old Sinbad to ruth was wrought
When, thus accosted for a lift,
A chronic pickaback he caught
From the old scrounger by the Drift.)

Then as I pondered this new trouble
Which he'd confided to my care,
Six others passed us, bending double,
Who seemed our fellowship to share –

For in their style was nothing alien,
Those Hyde Park Lancers,[159] dressed to stun,
In great cocked hats, with slouch Australian,
Though plume or chinstrap they had none.

Like grim knights-errant on their journey,
Couching their broomsticks tipped with pins,
I watched them joust their dismal tourney
Tentpegging garbage into tins.

Identically armed and hatted,
We prodded grimly as we bent:
No last-man-in has ever batted
With a more desperate intent.

---

[159] "The name given by soldiers to the Sanitary Scavengers of London County Council. They used to wear hats slightly resembling those worn by the author's regiment, the King's African Rifles, but without the bunch of feathers and the chinstrap." – Campbell's note.

In the same action were our talents
Employed, though in a different stead,
Since I was prodding for my balance
And they were prodding for their bread.

Gone was the thunder of great herds,
Lost was the lilt of marching men,
And void the bandolier[160] of words
That feeds the rifle of my pen.

I listened with my six companions
To the low hum of our environs
And London's streets, like roaring canyons,
With streams of whisky, blood and iron.

Amongst the leafless trees that froze
The wind struck up with flute and fife
The regimental march of those
Who've fallen out of step with life.

We must be silent when men mutter,
We must keep calm when tempers rise,
And when we're shoved into the gutter
It's we who must apologize.

To have one's Cross laid on inside
Abates no ardour in the strife
Though something in us might have died
Yet something more had come to life.

---

[160] Shoulder-belt with cartridge-loops.

Arion[161]

(To Mary Campbell)

Limping amongst the prams and bowlers
I dreamed that I had coursed in vain,
My dhow[162] the stallion of the rollers,
My horse the dolphin of the plain.
But you revive them. You refuse,
When by the fireside I would curl;
And with the ripe age of a Muse
Streamline the freshness of a girl,
To set the old momentum free,
To launch me into song, and be
My boat of roses, steed of fire,
At once the courser[163] and the shallop,[164]
The dolphin on whose surge I gallop,
The tune, the rapture, and the lyre!

---

[161] A Greek lyric poet of the seventh century B.C. Legend has it that on a sea journey the crew planned to murder him; they allowed him to sing one last time and threw him overboard, but a dolphin, attracted by the music, bore him up and carried him to shore.
[162] Oriental sailing craft.
[163] Swift horse.
[164] Light open boat.

Ska-hawtch Wha Hae!

A Likkle wee wee poom i'th' Ye Aulde Teashoppe Pidgin-Brogue, Lallands or Butter-Scotch (Wi' apooligees to MockDiarmid)[165]

'Twaa hoots for auld lamb swine, or new hog mutton,
Or young sheep ham! But, ha! Methinks he comes...'
                                  Shakes-
                                  Disappeare

Skwawtch wha hieland clanship braggis
Yet rides himsel' for want o' naggis
Whiles frae his chin a sporran waggis
        O' new-mown hay!
Skwawtch wha heehaw! Skwawtch wha haggis!
        Skwawtch wha hae!
Skwawtch wha heehaw-heehaw-hae!
Skwawtch wha heehaw doon the brae!
Skwawtch wha brainyell, bark, and bray
        In accents broader
And brogues more pidgin than the lay
        O' Harry Lauder![166]
Skwawtch wha bogus kinship claim
And plagiarize your thrice-worn frame
And third-hand kisser from Sir Jame'-
        -s Barrie[167] (the spit of him!)
And from a better man the name
        But not the wit of him!
His speech from graveyards long decayed
(While Burke and Hare[168] each downs his spade

---

[165] This poem was intended as an attack on Hugh MacDiarmid (1892-1978), Scottish poet and communist (expelled from the party, he rejoined in 1956, following the Russian occupation of Hungary), who was a founder member of the Scottish National Party. MacDiarmid championed the use of Scots dialect in poetry, often employing traditional or regional parochialisms in artificial and dubious contexts.
[166] Sir Harry Lauder (1870-1950), Scottish comedian and singer, a star of the Music Halls.
[167] Sir James Barrie (1860-1937), important Scottish dramatist and prose writer, author of delicate, beautifully constructed, rather sentimental plays, most famous for *Peter Pan*.
[168] Burke and Hare: infamous Edinburgh body snatchers whose activities formed the basis of stories by Robert Louis Stevenson and Dylan Thomas.

And holds his nose) – to learn their trade
              Might well enable
The International[169] Brigade,
              The men of Babel,
Or Uno's[170] imbecile convention
With something near their comprehension
And down their ears with dire intention
              That hellish brogue ram
With tidings from the Fourth Dimension
              Or the Fifth Programme.
Inventing vords vot's quite impossary,
Auld Skwawtch corrals them in the glossary
And so compiles a great What's-Whassery
              Of What is *Not*.
(When we for rhyme-ends at a loss are, he
              Is on the spot.)
For rhyme he cooks his spellings – say
As when *awaa'* becomes *away*:
He has it both ways, either way
              A lucky draw:
As here, converting "Skwawtch Wha hae"
              To "Skwawtch Wha Haw"!
Whatever ink he dips his pen in
Turns pink, as ven he vorships Lenin[171]
And hymns a prosty-toot who (when in
              Her trade the greedy puss
Takes him the millionth of her men in)
              Mothers his Oedipus.[172]
Till Auld Lamb Swine cried "Wait awee!"
(The floozie's chucker-out was he)
And Butter Skwawtch began to see
              Or think he saw

---

[169] The International Brigade was composed of volunteers from various countries who fought for the Republicans in the Spanish Civil War.

[170]

[171] McDiarmid had written two odes to Lenin.

[172] According to Greek legend, Oedipus, son of King Laius of Thebes, unknowingly killed his father and married his mother. When he realized what he had done, he put out his eyes. The subject of Sophocles's great play *Oedipus Rex*.

The difference between Skwawtch Wha Hee
    And Skwawtch Wha Haw.
'Twas Auld Lamb-Swine himsel' that morrn
Dressed only in his rat-hide sporr'n
Wha gied two toots upo' his horrn
    Sae cauld and clammie
That Butter Skwawtch was left forlorrn
    Wi'oot a Mammie.
"Lambswine, Lambswine, I'll hae the law,"
Cries Butter-Skwawtch, "hoots, mon, awa!" –
Lambswine he gies a loud guffaw
    And roared wi' glee,
While Butter-Skwawtch went "Skwawtch Wha Haw"
And "Skwawtch Wha Hee".
Skwawtch wha muddles up his syntax –
May Government his beer and gin tax!
Where'er he sits may there be tintacks
    To gall him wearier
Than if a caveman wi' a flint-axe
    Sawed his posterior.
May crabs devour his mangy sporran,
Make in his old rat's fur their warren
And clapper-claw his... Ghraidh Mho Horranh
    (I don't quite know
What that means, but this clear unforeign
    Footnote will show).[173]
So, Skwawtch wha heehaw heehaw hae!
Skwawtch wha heehaw doon the brae!
When burrdies cheep at blink o' day
    To catch the Wurrum,
Skwawtches wha go tae Bed – and stay!
    I much preferrum.

---

[173] "This is Butterscotch for *garbanzos* or chickpeas which all non bona-fide Highlanders are reputed to carry in their sporrans on long marches." – Campbell's note.

The Drummer Boy's Catechism
(An Essay in Hopkinese)[174]

Wagwanton man-chick, soldier-budlet, boyling
's soul needs grace more than his boots need oiling.
So comes he to the cleric (an
Orphan he is, whose sole aunt turned American).

Comes he to learn. Ah! visit now the tenth this is
To me, unworth. But in the mean parenthesis
Ah how ecstatic is m-
-y waiting soul with gust to hear his catechism!

His camp lies yonder. Yonder. His Camp-Commandant
Caught him and brought him. Nay! no false mahommedan t-
o blight this bud, or canker (chief
Server he is at mass). His pocket handkerchief

He into-wept, beseeching me to train him
In Godways, straitways, and his soul de-paynim.
(Deep pain him it would bring
Should soldier-budlet not with angels sing)

So Commandant (his name is Hector Braby)
Brings him half-hatched 'twixt angel-fledge and baby,
His soul a callow squeaker,
For shoulder-fitting and feather-fledging a seeker.

Both soul and bootsole squeak in need of oiling,
Unction, and clean ablution; boot and boyling
In trebles shrill compete,
Go "left-right-left", and end in a dead-heat.

---

[174] A Parody of Gerard Manley Hopkins (1884-1889), major British poet and Jesuit.

ROY CAMPBELL

Boots squeak at me, and uncracked voicelet hoots,
(What boots a squeak when squeakers wear the boots?)
Gold ringlets do his neck trick
Out in rich finery, silken-gingery-electric!

Youth-speckled, apple-freaked, dappled and peppered
With pimple, dimple, and freckle. Of beauty spots he's the leopard.
(Old Age, Ah blood-fierce hag you are,
Spare, spare, not deface, this galaxy-pimple-jaguar)

Of apricot splotches and birds-egg blotches. O spare 'im!
Egg of an angel, perhaps, is this harum scarum,
Wagwanton, weechappy –,
Spare him, and both myself and Commandant make happy.

Bumfluff on cheeks, like peach-down or penicillin
Blooms plushwise, 'twixt the pimples, space to fill in
With microscopic bristles
Finer, more fine (ah!) than silver tuft of thistles.

Due Overseas…Wilt roam (ah me!) redcoatlet?
Salvation I'll launch thee, which like a life-boatlet
I'll caulk. Yes! fore and aft let
No bilge soak in to sink thy spirit's raftlet,

But float, float, till boy be a buoy, a bell-buoy.
Boys will be buoys and with the angels dwell, boy.
(Poems and buoys are better for
The Hopkinese mis-mixture of a metaphor)

His catechism (which he not now garbles)
Buoys him, to beat the bugler-boy at marbles
I' the clash of alley and tor
And glassie, when back to camp he returns once more.

All the world over so-ever in rollround perimeter

Where on active service he's posted, – kris[175] nor scimitar
Pierce, nor assagai[176] quiver,
But miss by a mile, and egg-boy from danger deliver;

Egg-boy deliver, that angel may hatch from the oafy
Exterior shell; but spare me the shell as a trophy,
His photo to frame as it watches
Me counting its dimples and pimples and freckles and blotches.

Inscape[177] of Skytehawks on the Cookhouse Roof[178]

(In Homage to Gerard Manley Hopkins)

See! see the skytehawks perch, smelling the cookery, all in a rosary-rookery
Ranged, ranged in order, in file ranged, and, Ah! Oh! in rank ranged, on the topmost
Ridge o' the cookhouse roof. See, too, Rihambo, the cookboy, desist from his cookery
To fling a half-brick at them, fling a half-brick. That's when they flop most,
Flap, flop, and flounder i'th' air. Then they stop flopping; flop not, flap not, but stop most;
Yes, most of them stop flopping then! Then back to their perches they hop, most
Of them, back to their perches. Perches? Yes, perches. For each of them hops, hops, hops
Back, back to his perch. Yes perch! Not fish, but roof, where they drop most

---

[175] An elaborate oriental knife.
[176] Slender spear of hard wood used by South African tribes.
[177] Inscape: the metaphysical design, which gives a thing its beauty and reflects its essence or "thisness", according to Hopkins's reading of the philosophy of Duns Scotus.
[178] Another parody of Hopkins.

Most of their guano and whitewash. Now see, see, it's a half-
brick that one of them cops
Right on the kisser! A misser? No fear! fair and square on the
kisser he copped it,
Good work for the Company Cookboy, Rihambo! Give, give
him credit,
The Credit, oh, give, grant, and give him: since all that
rookery's ration-robbery of rotten cookery – he stopped it!
And all in a rosary-rookery, bead-bird-busted, those skytehawks
scatter for shelter –
Skytehawks scram in a scramble up-sky, scram in a scramble. A
scramble. You said it!
Raucous the caucus of the whole skytehawkery – and helter
they go in a skelter, helter-a-skelter.

San Juan de la Cruz[179]

When that brown bird, whose fusillading heart
Is triggered on a thorn the dark night through,
Has slain the only rival of his art
That burns, with flames for feathers, in the blue –
I think of him in whom those rivals met
To burn and sing, both bird and star, in one:
The planet slain, the nightingale would set
To leave a pyre of roses for the Sun.
His voice an iris through its rain of jewels –
Or are they tears, those embers of desire,
Whose molten brands each gust of song re-fuels? –
He crucifies his heart upon his lyre,
Phoenix of Song, whose deaths are his renewals,
With pollen for his cinders, bleeding fire!

---

[179] Written in May 1942 after Campbell had undergone basic army training in Wales. Since 1939, he had been reading and translating the poems of Saint John of the Cross, the great Spanish mystic and poet.

Upon a gloomy night
by St John of the Cross

Upon a gloomy night,
With all my cares to loving ardours flushed,
(O venture of delight!)
With nobody in sight
I went abroad when all my house was hushed.

In safety, in disguise,
In darkness up the secret stair I crept,
(O happy enterprise)
Concealed from other eyes
When all my house at length in silence slept.

Upon that lucky night
In secrecy, inscrutable to sight,
I went without discerning
And with no other light
Except for that which in my heart was burning.

It lit and led me through
More certain than the light of noonday clear
To where One waited near
Whose presence well I knew,
There where no other presence might appear.

Oh night that was my guide!
Oh darkness dearer than the morning's pride,
Oh night that joined the lover
To the beloved bride
Transfiguring them each into the other.

Within my flowering breast
Which only for himself entire I save
He sank into his rest
And all my gifts I gave
Lulled by the airs with which the cedars wave.

Over the ramparts fanned
While the fresh wind was fluttering his tresses,
With his serenest hand
My neck he wounded, and
Suspended every sense with its caresses.

Lost to myself I stayed
My face upon my lover having laid
From all endeavour ceasing:
And all my cares releasing
Threw them amongst the lilies there to fade.

Verses Written after an Ecstasy of High Exaltation
by St John of the Cross

I entered in, I know not where,
And I remained, though knowing naught,
Transcending knowledge with my thought.

Of when I entered I know naught,
But when I saw that I was there
(Though where it was I did not care)
Strange things I learned, with greatness fraught.
Yet what I heard I'll not declare.
But there I stayed, though knowing naught,
Transcending knowledge with my thought.

Of peace and piety interwound
This perfect science had been wrought,
Within the solitude profound
A straight and narrow path it taught,
Such secret wisdom there I found
That there I stammered, saying naught,
But topped all knowledge with my thought.

So borne aloft, so drunken-reeling,
So rapt was I, so swept away,
Within the scope of sense or feeling
My sense or feeling could not stay.
And in my soul I felt, revealing,
A sense that, though its sense was naught,
Transcended knowledge with my thought.

The man who truly there has come
Of his own self must shed the guise;
Of all he knew before the sum
Seems far beneath that wondrous prize:
And in this lore he grows so wise
That he remains, though knowing naught,
Transcending knowledge with his thought.

The farther that I climbed the height
The less I seemed to understand
The cloud so tenebrous and grand
That there illuminates the night.
For he who understands that sight
Remains for aye, though knowing naught,
Transcending knowledge with his thought.

This wisdom without understanding.
Is of so absolute a force
No wise man of whatever standing
Can ever stand against its course,
Unless they tap its wondrous source,

To know so much, though knowing naught,
They pass all knowledge with their thought.

This summit all so steeply towers
And is of excellence so high
No human faculties or powers
Can ever to the top come nigh.
Whoever with its steep could vie,
Though knowing nothing, would transcend
All thought, forever, without end.

If you would ask, what is its essence –
This summit of all sense and knowing:
It comes from the Divinest Presence –
The sudden sense of Him outflowing,
In His great clemency bestowing
The gift that leaves men knowing naught,
Yet passing knowledge with their thought.

Coplas[180] *about the Soul which Suffers with Impatience to See God*
by St John of the Cross

I live without inhabiting
Myself – in such a wise that I
Am dying that I do not die.

Within myself I do not dwell
Since without God I cannot live.
Reft of myself, and God as well,
What serves this life (I cannot tell)
Except a thousand deaths to give?
Since waiting here for life I lie
And die because I do not die.

---

[180] Verses.

This life I live in vital strength
Is loss of life unless I win You:
And thus to die I shall continue
Until in You I live at length.
Listen (my God!) my life is in You.
This life I do not want, for I
Am dying that I do not die.

Thus in your absence and your lack
How can I in myself abide
Nor suffer here a death more black
Than ever was by mortal died.
For pity of myself I've cried
Because in such a plight I lie
Dying because I do not die.

The fish that from the stream is lost
Derives some sort of consolation
That in his death he pays the cost
At least of death's annihilation.
To this dread life with which I'm crossed
What fell death can compare, since I,
The more I live, the more must die.

When thinking to relieve my pain
I in the sacraments behold You
It brings me greater grief again
That to myself I cannot fold You.
And that I cannot see you plain
Augments my sorrows, so that I
Am dying that I do not die

If in the hope I should delight,
Oh Lord, of seeing You appear,
The thought that I might lose Your sight,
Doubles my sorrow and my fear.
Living as I do in such fright,
And yearning as I yearn, poor I
Must die because I do not die.

Oh rescue me from such a death
My God, and give me life, not fear;
Nor keep me bound and struggling here
Within the bonds of living breath.
Look how I long to see You near,
And how in such a plight I lie
Dying because I do not die!

I shall lament my death betimes,
And mourn my life, that it must be
Kept prisoner by sins and crimes
So long before I am set free:
Ah God, my God, when shall it be?
When I may say (and tell no lie)
I live because I've ceased to die?

Concerning Christ and the Soul
by St John of the Cross

A shepherd lad was mourning his distress,
Far from all comfort, friendless and forlorn.
He fixed his thought upon his shepherdess
Because his breast by love was sorely torn.

He did not weep that love had pierced him so,
Nor with self-pity that the shaft was shot,
Though deep into his heart had sunk the blow,
It grieved him more that he had been forgot.

Only to think that he had been forgotten
By his sweet shepherdess, with travail sore,
He let his foes (in foreign lands begotten)
Gash the poor breast that love had gashed before.

"Alas! Alas! for him," the Shepherd cries,
"Who tries from me my dearest love to part
So that she does not gaze into my eyes
Or see that I am wounded to the heart."

Then, after a long time, a tree he scaled,
Opened his strong arms bravely wide apart,
And clung upon that tree till death prevailed,
So sorely was he wounded in his heart.

Song of the Soul that is glad to know God by Faith
by St John of the Cross

How well I know that fountain's rushing flow
Although by night

Its deathless spring is hidden. Even so
Full well I guess from whence its sources flow
Though it be night.

Its origin (since it has none) none knows:
But that all origin from it arose
Although by night.

I know there is no other thing so fair
And earth and heaven drink refreshment there
Although by night.

Full well I know its depth no man can sound
And that no ford to cross it can be found
Though it be night.

Its clarity unclouded still shall be:
Out of it comes the light by which we see
Though it be night.

Flush with its banks the stream so proudly swells;
I know it waters nations, heavens, and hells
Though it be night.

The current that is nourished by this source
I know to be omnipotent in force
Although by night.

From source and current a new current swells
Which neither of the other twain excels
Though it be night.

The eternal source hides in the Living Bread
That we with life eternal may be fed
Though it be night.

Here to all creatures it is crying, hark!
That they should drink their fill though in the dark,
For it is night.

This living fount which is to me so dear
Within the bread of life I see it clear
Though it be night.

Romance
Of the communion of the three Persons
by St John of the Cross

Out of the love immense and bright
That from the two had thus begun,
Words of ineffable delight
The Father spoke unto the Son:

Words of so infinite a rapture
Their drift by none could be explained:
Only the Son their sense could capture
That only to Himself pertained.

What of them we can sense the clearest
Was in this manner said and thought:
Out of Your company, my Dearest,
I can be satisfied by nought.

But if aught please me, I as duly
In You, Yourself, the cause construe.
The one who satisfies Me truly
Is him who most resembles You.

He who in nought resembles You
Shall find of Me no trace or sign,
Life of My Life! for only through
Your own can I rejoice in Mine.

You are the brilliance of My light
My wisdom and My power divine,
The figure of My substance bright
In whom I am well pleased to shine!

The man who loves You, O my Son,
To him Myself I will belong.
The love that in Yourself I won

I'll plant in him and root it strong,
Because he loved the very one
I loved so deeply and so long.

On Lisi's Golden Hair

(Translated for Edith Sitwell[181])
by Quevedo[182]

When you shake loose your hair from all controlling,
Such thirst of beauty quickens my desire
Over its surge in red tornadoes rolling
My heart goes surfing on the waves of fire.
Leander[183], who for love the tempest dares,
It lets a sea of flames its life consume:
Icarus[184], from a sun whose rays are hairs,
Ignites its wings and glories in its doom.
Charring its hopes (whose deaths I mourn) it strives
Out of their ash to fan new phoenix-lives
That, dying of delight, new hopes embolden.
Miser, yet poor, the crime and fate it measures
Of Midas[185], starved and mocked with stacks of treasures,
Or Tantalus[186], with streams that shone as golden.

---

[181] Dame Edith Sitwell (1887-1964), important experimental poet, critic and eccentric, and friend and admirer of Campbell's.

[182] Francisco Gomez de Quevedo y Villagas (1580-1645), a great Spanish satirist and poet, much admired by Byron.

[183] A Greek mythological figure who drowned swimming the Hellespont to keep a tryst with his love, Her

[184] Greek mythological figure who fell from the skies when, trying to escape from the labyrinth with his father Daedalus on wings the latter had made from wax and feathers, he flew too close to the sun and the wax melted.

[185] Mythic Greek king: all he touched turned to gold including, ultimately, his food and his daughter.

[186] Mythic Greek king who was punished in Hades by the gods for serving them his son in a stew: chained in water up to his chin, under the boughs of an apple tree, he was perpetually tantalized by the food he could not eat and the water he could not drink.

Counsel
by Bandeira[187]

The world is pitiless and lewdly jeers
All tragedy. Anticipate your loss.
Weep silently, in secret. Hide your tears,
So to become accustomed to your cross.

Alone grief can ennoble us. She only
Is grand and pure. Then learn to love her now –
To be your muse, when you are left and lonely,
And lay the last green laurels on your brow.

She will be sent from Heaven. The seraphic
Language she speaks in, you should learn, for she
Can talk no other in your daily traffic

When you receive her to replace your bride.
Pray humbly, too, to God, that she may be
A constant, kind companion at your side.

The Shadow of My Soul
by Federico Garcia Lorca[188]

The shadow of my soul
Flees down a sunset of alphabets
Foggy with books
And words.

The shadow of my soul!

---

[187] A Brazilian poet (1886-?). Translated from the Portuguese.
[188] Federico García Lorca (1899-1936), major Spanish poet and dramatist. He was executed in mysterious circumstances by Nationalist forces in the Spanish Civil War. Campbell translated many of his poems and plays, and also wrote a book about him.

I've come to the line where nostalgia
Ceases,
And the drip of lamentation turns
Into the alabaster of the spirit.

The shadow of my soul.

A flake of grief
Fades away,
But the reason and the substance remain
Of my old noon of lips,
Of my old noon
Of glances.

The shadow of my soul!

And a hallucination
Controls my gaze.
I see the word love
Crumbled away.

My nightingale!
Nightingale!
Are you still singing?

Rain
by Lorca

Rain has a vague and secret tenderness
Something of drowsiness resigned and lovable.
A humble music wakes with it, that makes
The drowsy spirit of the land vibrate.

It's a blue kiss which the Earth receives,
The primitive myth that's realized once more.
The contact already cold of the old sky and the earth
With a meekness of constant nightfall approaching.

It's the daybreak of the fruit. That which brings flowers
And anoints us with the holy spirit of the seas.
That which pours out life on the sown fields
And into the soul, the sorrow of what it doesn't know.

The terrible nostalgia of a wasted life.
The fatal sense of being born too late.
Oh the restless illusion of an impossible tomorrow
With the near certitude of pain of the flesh,

Love wakens in the greyness of its rhythm,
Our interior heaven has a triumph of blood,
But our hope turns to sorrow
Seeing the drops lie dead upon the panes.

And the drops are – the eyes of the infinite that gaze
To the white infinity that is their mother.

Each drop of rain trembles on the dim pane
And leaves it with divine wounds of diamond.
It's the poets of the rain who've seen and meditate
What the crowd of rivers know nothing about.

Oh Silent rain, without storms or gusts,
Rain mild and serene with cattle-bells and soft light,
Rain peaceful and good, who are the true one,
That falls loving and sad over all things.

Franciscan rain who raise to form your drops
The souls of fountains dear and humble rills,
When on the land thus slowly you descend,
You open up roses in my breast with your sound.

The primitive song that you sing to the silence,
The sonorous story you tell to the boughs –
My lonely heart comments upon them weeping
In a deep black pentagram without a key.

My heart holds the sorrow of the serene rain,
The resigned sorrow of an unrealizable thing.
I have a star lit on the horizon
But my heart prevents me from running to see it.

Oh silent rain, beloved of the trees,
Who are so moving a sweetness on the piano.
You give to the soul the same mists and sounds
That you give to the drowsy soul of the land.

The Song of the Honey
by Lorca

Honey is the word of Christ.
The molten gold of his love.
It is beyond nectar,
The mummia[189] of the light of paradise.

---

[189] Bitumen (from the Arabic *mumiyah*). It was widely believed that Egyptian mummies were prepared with bitumen, which was supposed to have medicinal value and was sold in

The hive is a chaste star,
A well of amber fed by the rhythm
Of the bees. A breast of the fields
Trembling with fragrances and humming sounds.

Honey is the epic poem of love,
The materialization of the infinite.
The soul and the suffering blood of the flowers
Condensed in passing through another soul.

(Thus the honey of mankind is poetry
Which flows from his wounded breast,
From a honeycomb, whose wax is memory,
Formed by the bee of intimacy)

Honey is the pastoral poem
Of the shepherd, the flute, and the olive tree,
The brother of the milk and the acorn,
Supreme queens of the golden century.

Honey is like the sun of the morning
With all the charm of summer
And the ancient coolness of Autumn.
It is the withered leaf and the corn.

Oh divine liquor of humility
Serene as a primitive verse!

You are harmony made flesh.
The summary of all lyrical genius.
Within you slumber melancholy,
The secret of kisses, and of the cry.

---

apothecary's shops in the Middle Ages, made from pounding mummified bodies. i.e. an elixir of life.

Most sweet. Sweet. That's your adjective.
Sweet as the belly of women.
Sweet as the eyes of children.
Sweet as the shade of night.
Sweet as a voice.

                Or as a lily.

For him who carries sorrow and the lyre
You are the sun which lights him on his way.
You equal every form of beauty
Of colour, light, and sound.

Oh divine liquor of hope
Where in the perfection of equilibrium
Spirit and matter arrive in unity,
As in the Host the blood and light of Christ.

And the higher soul is that of the flowers.
Oh liquor which has blended all these souls!
He who tastes you little knows that he swallows
The golden summary of all lyricism.

Elegy
by Lorca

Like a censer full of desires
You pass in the clear and luminous afternoon
With the dim flesh of a faded lily
And your sex powerful in your glance.

You wear your mouth the melancholy
Of dead purity, and on the dionysiac
Snowdrift of your belly you bear the spider that weaves
The barren web that covers a womb
Which never flowered with the living roses
Which are the fruit of kisses.

              In your white hands
You carry the skein of your illusions,
Dead forever, and bear in your spirit,
Your Passion, hungry for kisses of fire,
And the mother-love, which dreams remote visions
Of cradles and domestic peace
Threading your lips with the azure of lullabies.

Like Ceres[190] you would give your sheaves of gold
If drowsy love were once to touch your body,
And like the Virgin Mary from your breasts
You could spout forth another milky way.

You will wither like a magnolia.
Nobody will kiss your thighs of fire,
Nor to your tresses will arrive the fingers
That would vibrate them
                like the strings of a lyre.

Oh powerful woman of ebony and nard,[191]
Whose breath has the whiteness of biznagas[192]
Venus with the Manila shawl who tastes of
The wine of Malaga and the guitar.

Oh swarthy swan, whose lake has waterlilies
Of saetas,[193] waves of oranges,
And red foam of carnations that perfume
The faded nests that are beneath your wings.

...

---

[190] The Roman goddess of the harv
[191] (A Plant yielding) aromatic balsam of the ancient
[192] Statuesque giant cactus.
[193] Something given to the beloved: Cupid's dart, a song etc. (Spanish).

But the rings grow wider round your eyes
And your black hair to silver goes on turning;
Your breasts slip down pouring their fragrance forth,
And your splendid back begins to stoop.

Oh slender, maternal, and burning woman!
Dolorous virgin who have been pierced
By all the stars in the deep sky
Through a heart already without hope.

You are the mirror of an Andalusia
Which suffers giant passions, yet is silent.
Passions that sway in fans
And in mantillas over the white throats
Which are trembling with blood, with snow,
And the red scratches which are made by glances.

You go through the mists of autumn, virgin
As Agnes, Cecilia, or the sweet Saint Clare,
Though you're a bacchante who might have danced
Crowned with green buds and vines.

The vast sorrow which floats in your eyes
Tells us the broken failure of your life,
The monotony of the poor life you lead
Watching people pass from your window,
Hearing the rain fall on the bitterness
Of the old provincial street,
While in the distance sounds the uproar,
Turbulent and confused, of bells.

But in vain you listen to the accents of the wind.
The sweet serenade will never reach your ears.
From behind your panes you still watch eagerly.
What a deep sorrow you will have in your soul
To feel in your weary and exhausted breast
The passion of a young girl newly fallen in love!

Your body will go to the tomb
Intact of all emotions.
Over the dark earth
Will break the dawn.
From your eyes will come two blood-red carnations.
And from your breasts roses as white as snow.
But your great sorrow will rise to the stars,
As another star worthy to wound and eclipse them.

Merry-go-round
by Lorca

The days of feasts
Revolve on wheels.
The merry-go-round brings them
And takes them away.

Blue day of Corpus.
White Christmas Eve.

The days discard
Their skins, like snakes,
With the exception
Of the days of feasts.

These are the same
As our old mothers.
Their evenings are long trains
Of silk and sequins.

Blue day of Corpus.
White Christmas Eve.

The merry-go-round revolves

Ranging from a star.
Tulip of the five
Divisions of the world.

Or little horses,
Disguised as panthers,
Children devour the moon
As if it were a cherry.

Frenzy! Frenzy! Marco Polo!
On a fantastic wheel,
The children see the undiscovered
Remoteness of the earth.

Blue day of Corpus.
White Christmas Eve.

They Cut Down Three Trees
by Lorca

There were three.
(The day came with its axes.)
There were two.
(Trailing wings of silver.)
There was one.
There were none.
(The water was left naked.)

ROY CAMPBELL

Benediction
by Charles Baudelaire[194]

When by an edict of the powers supreme
A poet's born into this world's drab space,
His mother starts, in horror, to blaspheme
Clenching her fists at God, who grants her grace.

"Would that a nest of vipers I'd aborted
Rather than this absurd abomination.
Cursed be the night of pleasures vainly sported
On which my womb conceived my expiation.

Since of all women I am picked by You
To be my Mate's aversion and his shame:
And since I cannot, like a *billet-doux*,
Consign this stunted monster to the flame,

I'll turn the hatred, which You load on me,
On the curst tool through which You work your spite,
And twist and stunt this miserable tree
Until it cannot burgeon for the blight."

She swallows down the white froth of her ire
And, knowing naught of schemes that are sublime,
Deep in Gehenna,[195] starts to lay the pyre
That's consecrated to maternal crime.

---

[194] Charles Baudelaire (1821-1867), major French poet. "Having had considerable success with my translation of a Saint, Saint John of the Cross, I determined to translate a fellow-sinner who is hardly less a believer, even in his rebellious and blasphemous moments, than the Saint himself. I have been reading Baudelaire since I was fifteen, carried him in my haversack through two wars, and have loved him longer and more deeply than any other poet. I translated Saint John of the Cross because he miraculously saved my life in Toledo in 1936. I am translating Baudelaire because he lived my life up to the same age, with similar sins, remorses, ostracisms, and poverty and the same desperate hope of reconciliation and pardon..." – Campbell's note.
[195] Hell.

Yet with an unseen Angel for protector
The outcast waif grows drunken with the sun,
And finds ambrosia, too, and rosy nectar
In all he eats or drinks, suspecting none.

He sings upon his *Via Crucis*,[196] plays
With winds, and with the clouds exchanges words:
The Spirit following his pilgrim-ways
Weeps to behold him gayer than the birds.

Those he would love avoid him as in fear,
Or, growing bold to see one so resigned,
Compete to draw from him a cry or tear,
And test on him the fierceness of their kind.

In food or drink that's destined for his taste
They mix saliva foul with cinders black,
Drop what he's touched with hypocrite distaste,
And blame themselves for walking in his track.

His wife goes crying in the public way
–"Since fair enough he finds me to adore,
The part of ancient idols I will play
And gild myself with coats of molten ore.

I will get drunk on incense, myrrh, and nard,
On genuflexions, meat, and heady wine.
Out of his crazed and wondering regard,
I'll laugh to steal prerogatives divine.

When by such impious farces bored at length,
I'll place my frail strong hand on him, and start,
With nails like those of harpies in their strength,
To plough myself a pathway to his heart.

---

[196] Way of the Cross.

Like a young bird that trembles palpitating,
I'll wrench his heart, all crimson, from his chest,
And to my favourite beast, his hunger sating,
Will fling it in the gutter with a jest."

Skyward, to where he sees a Throne blaze splendid,
The pious Poet lifts his arms on high,
And the vast lightnings of his soul extended
Blot out the crowds and tumults from his eye.

"Blessèd be You, O God, who give us pain,
As cure for our impurity and wrong –
Essence that primes the stalwart to sustain
Seraphic raptures that were else too strong.

I know that for the Poet You've a post,
Where the blest Legions take their ranks and stations,
Invited to the revels with the host
Of Virtues, Powers, and Thrones, and Dominations.[197]

That grief's the sole nobility, I know it,
Where neither Earth nor Hell can make attacks,
And that, to deck my mystic crown of poet,
All times and universes paid their tax.

But all the gems from old Palmyra[198] lost,
The ores unmixed, the pearls of the abyss,
Set by Your hand, could not suffice the cost
Of such a blazing diadem as this.

---

[197] Orders of angels.
[198] City of Palms, "The Rome of the East", seat of the fabled Queen Zenobia (3rd century A.D.).

Because it will be only made of light,
Drawn from the hearth of the essential rays,
To which our mortal eyes, when burning bright,
Are but the tarnished mirrors that they glaze."

I love the thought of those old naked days
by Baudelaire

I love the thought of those old naked days
When Phoebus gilded torsos with his rays,
When men and women sported, strong and fleet,
Without anxiety or base deceit,
And heaven caressed them, amorously keen
To prove the health of each superb machine.
Cybele[199] then was lavish of her guerdon
And did not find her sons too gross a burden:
But, like a she-wolf, in her love great-hearted,
Her full brown teats to all the world imparted.
Bold, handsome, strong, Man rightly might evince
Pride in the glories that proclaimed him prince –
Fruits pure of outrage, by the blight unsmitten,
With firm, smooth flesh that cried out to be bitten.

Today the Poet, when he would assess
Those native splendours in the nakedness
Of man or woman, feels a sombre chill
Enveloping his spirit and his will.
He meets a gloomy picture, which he loathes,
Wherein deformity cries out for clothes.
Oh comic runts! Oh horror of burlesque!
Lank, flabby, skewed, pot-bellied, and grotesque!
Whom their smug god, Utility (poor brats!)
Has swaddled in his brazen clouts "ersatz"

---

[199] Mother of the gods, goddess of fecundity.

As with cheap tinsel. Women tallow-pale,
Both gnawed and nourished by debauch, who trail
The heavy burden of maternal vice,
Or of fecundity the hideous price.

We have (corrupted nations) it is true
Beauties the ancient people never knew –
Sad faces gnawed by cancers of the heart
And charms which morbid lassitudes impart.
But these inventions of our tardy muse
Can't force our ailing peoples to refuse
Just tribute to the holiness of youth
With its straightforward mien, its forehead couth,
The limpid gaze, like running water bright,
Diffusing, careless, through all things, like the light
Of azure skies, the birds, the winds, the flowers
The songs, and perfumes, and heart-warming powers.

The Carcase
by Baudelaire

The object that we saw, let us recall,
This summer morn when warmth and beauty mingle –
At the path's turn, a carcase lay asprawl
      Upon a bed of shingle.

Legs raised, like some old whore far-gone in passion,
The burning, deadly, poison-sweating mass
Opened its paunch in careless, cynic fashion,
      Ballooned with evil gas.

On this putrescence the sun blazed in gold,
Cooking it to a turn with eager care –
So to repay to Nature, hundredfold,
      What she had mingled there.

The sky, as on the opening of a flower,
On this superb obscenity smiled bright.
The stench drove at us, with such fearsome power
      You thought you'd swoon outright.

Flies trumpeted upon the rotten belly
Whence larvae poured in legions far and wide,
And flowed, like molten and liquescent jelly,
      Down living rags of hide.

The mass ran down, or, like a wave elated
Rolled itself on, and crackled as if frying:
You'd think that corpse, by vague breath animated,
      Drew life from multiplying.

Through that strange world a rustling rumour ran
Like rushing water or a gust of air,
Or grain that winnowers, with rhythmic fan,
      Sweep simmering here and there.

It seemed a dream after the forms grew fainter,
Or like a sketch that slowly seems to dawn
On a forgotten canvas, which the painter
      From memory has drawn.

Behind the rocks a restless cur that slunk
Eyed us with fretful greed to recommence
His feast, amidst the bonework, on the chunk
      That he had torn from thence.

Yet you'll resemble this infection too
One day, and stink and sprawl in such a fashion,
Star of my eyes, sun of my nature, you,
      My angel and my passion!

Yes, you must come to this, O queen of graces,
At length, when the last sacraments are over,
And you go down to moulder in dark places
    Beneath the grass and clover.

Then tell the vermin as it takes its pleasure
And feasts with kisses on that face of yours,
I've kept intact in form and godlike essence
    Our decomposed amours!

The Duel
by Baudelaire

Two fighters rushed together: sabres bleak
With crimson blood-gouts lit the air above.
That clinking swordplay was the tender squeak
Of youth, when it's a prey to bleating love.

The swords are splintered, like our youth, my darling,
And now it's teeth and talons are the fashion.
The clash of swords is child's play to the snarling
Of hearts adult in ulcerated passion.

In the ravine by lynx and leopard haunted,
Our heroes, wrestling heroes, roll undaunted.
Rags of their skin flower red upon the gorse.

This gulf is hell, and peopled by our friends.
Here, hellcat! Come, let's roll without remorse
To celebrate a feud that never ends!

SELECTED POEMS

Drunken Boat
by Arthur Rimbaud[200]

I felt no more the guidance of my tow-men
As I came down by listless river-coasts.
To serve for targets, whooping Redskin bowmen
Had pinned them naked to their coloured posts.

Bearer of Flemish corn or English cotton,
I cared no more for crews of any kind.
When with my own the scuffle was forgotten,
The rivers let me rove as I inclined.

Into the furious chopping of the tides
Last winter, heedless as a child, I glided;
Nor have the unmoored headlands on their sides
Sustained so proud a buffeting as I did.

The Storm had blessed my watches in the spray:
Cork-light I danced the waves for ten whole nights
(Those everlasting maulers of their prey!)
Nor missed the foolish blink of harbour-lights.

Sweet, as to children the tart flesh of apples,
Green water pierced my shell with juicy shudder,
Spewing a wine of azure blots and dapples
That rinsed me round, dispersing helm and rudder.

Since then I have gone bathing in the hymn
Of a sea sprayed with stars and whitely creaming:
Devouring the green depths where, flotsam dim,
Sometimes a drowning man descends half-dreaming:

---

[200] Arthur Rimbaud (1854-1891), major French symbolist poet who wrote all his poems in his youth.

Where with slow-pulsing and delirious fires,
To flush the blue, while day blazed white above,
Stronger than wine and vaster than your lyres,
Ferments the crimson bitterness of love.

I've known the surf, the waterspouts, the tide:
Lightning-split skies: the dusk: the dawn upheld
Like a whole swarm of doves; and I have spied
Sometimes, what Man believes he has beheld.

Lighting long wisps in violent panoramas,
I have seen mystic horrors scrawl the sun:
Far waves, like actors in the ancient dramas,
Unroll their flickering shutters as they run.

I've dreamed the green night lit with dazzling frost
A kiss that to the sea's eyes slowly grew,
The flow of saps to human knowledge lost,
And singing phosphorescence gold and blue.

Like mad stampedes of cattle on the prairies,
With breakers I have charged the reefs and screes[201]
For months: nor dreamed the lit feet of the Maries
Could force a snaffle of those snorting seas.

Blurring with flowers the eyes of human leopards,
I've whirled Floridas none yet set eyes on,
Where, stretching coloured reins, the Iris shepherds
Her glaucous[202] flocks beneath the sea's horizon.

I've seen the swamps ferment, huge creels of rushes,
Where rots a whole Leviathan as it sleeps,
Amidst dead calms collapsing water-gushes,
And distances cascading to the deeps:

---

[201] Small stones covering a mountain slope that slide down when trodden underfoot.
[202] Of dull greyish green or blue.

Glaciers, white suns, pearl waves, skies of red coals:
At limits of brown gulfs, foul objects stranded:
Where huge bug-eaten snakes from twisted boles
Fell dying with black perfumes where they landed.

I would have shown those bream of the blue billow
To children, those gold fish, those fish that sing;
Foam flowers for my escape have smoothed a pillow
And winds ineffable have waved my wing.

Tired martyr, round the poles and tropics rolled,
The wave, whose sobs my cradle rocked at ease,
Raised flowers of shade with spiracles of gold
And left me like a woman on her knees.

Half-island, tilting at my sides the frays
And tail-shots of the blond-eyed birds that scream,
I wandered, while across my flimsy stays
Drowned men descended backwards down to dream.

Lost in the hair of coves or like a shaft
Shot into birdless ether, I, lost boat,
Whose sea-drunk corpse no Hanseatic craft
Nor monitor could salvage or refloat,

Free, smoking, by the violet fog embraced,
Have broached the sky's red wall and bored it through,
Which bears, so dainty to good poets' taste,
Lichens of sun, and mucus of the blue.

Scribbled with small electric moons, mad plank,
With black sea-horses harnessed to my gunnels,[203]
I've run, while Summer bashed to dust, and sank
The jet-blue sky to swirl down blazing funnels,

---

[203] The Upper edge of a ship's or boat's

I who have quaked to hear, at fifty leagues,
The rut of Behemoths[204] and Maelstroms roar,
Threader of endless calms whom naught fatigues,
Am sick for Europe's towers of ancient lore.

Starred archipelagos I've seen and islands
Where maddening skies, to tempt the rover, flower,
Where hide you in those nights of topless silence
(Millions of golden birds!) predestined Power?

But, true, I've wept too much. The dawns are fearful.
Each moon is loathsome. Suns are sour to me.
Salt love has bloated me and sogged me tearful.
May my keel splinter! Give me to the sea!

If there's a northern water that I crave,
It's the black slush, at scented close of day,
Whereon a child releases, sadly grave,
A boat frail as the butterflies of May.

No more, bathed in your languor, waves! I'll trim
Her seawake where the cotton-clipper flies:
Nor cross the pomp of flags and flames: nor swim
Beneath the convict-hulks' resentful eyes.

---

[204] Enormous beast.

The thing that hurts and wrings
by Fernando Pessoa[205]

The thing that hurts and wrings
Was never in my heart.
It's one of those fair things
In life that have no part.

Shapes without shape – each shape
Seems silently to flit
Ere known by grief, and fade
Ere love can dream of it.

They are as if our grief
Were a dark tree from whom
They flutter leaf by leaf
Into the mist and gloom.

Death comes before its time
by Pessoa

Death comes before its time,
Life is so brief a stay.
Each moment is the mime
Of what is lost for aye.

---

[205] Fernando Pessoa (1888-1935), major Portuguese poet and prose writer, born in Durban of Jewish extraction. An Anglophile who often wrote in English. He wrote under three heteronyms beside his proper name – Alberto Caerio, Ricardo Reis and Alvaro dos Campos – each one representing a different aspect of his personality, each with a different style and a different identity, as if he were four different poets. "Campos" sang the epic of the Portuguese soul in free verse, while "Pessoa's" poems were written in traditional metres and strict rhyme.

Life scarcely had begun,
Nor the idea diminished,
When he whose task was done
Knew not what he had finished.

This, doubting Death presumes
To cancel and to cut
out of the book of dooms,
Which God forgot to shut.

The poet fancying each belief
by Pessoa

The poet fancying each belief
So wholly through and through
Ends by imagining the grief
He really feels is true.

And those who read what he has spelt
In the read grief feel good –
Not in the two griefs he has felt,
But one they never could.

Thus to beguile and entertain
The reason, does he start,
Upon its rails, the clockwork train
That's also called the heart.

From *The Maritime Ode*
by Campos[206]

The whole quay is a memory in stone.
And when the ship leaves it, and suddenly
One sees the space widen
Between the quay and the ship,
I feel, I know not why, a recent anguish,
A haze of mournful feeling,
That shines in the sun of my grief
Like the first pane on which the morning shimmers.
It clothes me in the memory of another being
Whose person was mysteriously mine.

Who knows? Who knows if I have never
Embarked before, myself, from such a quay?
As a ship in the oblique rays of the morning sun, who knows
If I have not sailed from a different kind of port?
Who knows if I have not left (before the time
Of this exterior world as I behold it
Striping itself with colours for my sake)
A great Quay filled with the fewness of the people
Of as vast, as distended and apoplectic a city
As can exist outside of Space and Time.

Yes... from a quay in some way material,
Visible as a quay, real, and truly a quay,
The absolute Quay, from whose model, unconsciously were copied,
And insensibly evoked,
All the quays of our ports,
Our quays of actual stone in actual water,
Which, once constructed, announce themselves
As Real-Things, Spirit-Things, or Entities of the Stone-Soul,
Made ours at certain moments by root-sensations,

---

[206] Alternative identity of Pessoa's.

When in the outer world, as if a door were opened,
But altering nothing,
The All in its diversity is shown.

Ah, the great quay from which we sailed as Nation Ships!
The great Anterior Quay, eternal and divine!
From what port? In what waters? (Or else, how could I think it?)
A great Quay, like the others, but uniquely *the* Quay,
Filled, like the rest, with rustling silences before the dawn,
And unwinding at daybreak in a roar of cranes and winches,
With trains arriving full of merchandise
Under the occasional, light cloud
Of smoke from nearby factories,
Which shadows its floor
Black with sequinned atoms that twinkle
As if it were the shade of a dark cloud
Passing over the face of black water.

After Rubén Darío[207]

One day an earthquake seemed to pass
I felt, with sudden dread,
As if a Babel made of glass
Were splintering in my head.

With Pascal's travelling abyss
I've toured: with Baudelaire
Have felt the wing of madness hiss
And graze my standing hair.

---

[207] Rubén Darío (1867-1916), the great Nicaraguan poet, short story writer and critic, the father of modern Spanish poetry.

I know the insect in the ointment,
The weevil in the bread,
The eternal ache of disappointment
To all achievement wed.

I whittled up my pens like sticks
And ribboned them with rhyme:
Like banderillas[208] to transfix
The changing hump of time.

But one must win at any price
And fight, to the last breath,
To be the Conqueror of Vice,
Of Madness, and of Death.

Nativity

All creatures then rejoiced, save that the Seven
   Capital steers of whom I am a herder
      (My Cloven heart their hoofprint in the mire)
With bloodshot glare interrogated heaven,
   And, back to back, with lowered horns of murder
      From spiracles of fury spitted fire.

Never so joyfully the brave cocks crew –
   No more by turns, but all with one accord.
      Never so early woke the mule and ox
Since it was day before the east was blue:
   Mary was dawn, the Sunrise was our Lord,
      And Joseph was the watchtower on the rocks.

---

[208] In a bullfight, the decorated darts thrust into the bull's neck or shoulders before the kill by the banderilleros.

Never for such a golden quilt lay blooming
   The fields, as for this richly-laden hay,
      And though the frost was sharp before the day,
The mule and ox, whose respiration fuming
   Ignited in the lantern's dim, red ray,
      Warmed him with rosy feathers where he lay.

Far overhead streamed on the signal meteor,
   The Ariadne[209] of the maps, who slowly
      Unwound the light and reeled the darkness up.
Love filled with fierce delight the humblest creature
   As heaven fills an eye, or as the Holy
      Infinitude the wafer and the cup.

Shepherds and kings and cowboys knelt around
   And marvelled that, while they could feel the power
      Whose rapture roars in God, yet God should moan:
And while His glory raised men off the ground
   (For Eve had brought such jewels in her dower)
      The tears of man should shine in God alone.

Autobiography in Fifty Kicks

If you hear of my death, do not worry two hoots.
It will mean that Existence is changing its boots.
For my lot is the football's, in pleasure or strife,
Addicted to getting a kick out of life.
The first kick I had was my grandmother's gift,
The kick of a rifle I scarcely could lift,
When the great Kudu-bull[210] saw the last of his days
And hunter and quarry were skittled both ways,

---

[209] Daughter of King Minos of Crete. She fell in love with Theseus and enabled him to defeat the Minotaur by providing him with a thread which led him through the Labyrinth and out again.
[210] The kudu is one of the most striking and beautiful of the antelopes.

The next kick I got from the rod in my hold,
As through the green water the mullet I trolled,
And the shark, like a maid unsuspecting her fate,
Turned up his white belly to swallow the bait –
And a terror to hold was the shrieking bamboo
When the fighting sea-tiger had buckled it to!
The next I received when the plaza was full,
The kick of a lance in the hump of a bull.
But then I got one from a hoof of the Devil
And it took me a couple of years to get level,
When down went his headpiece, and up went his tail,
As the fire-banderillas roared out on the gale!
Then the kick of a bronco that bounced like a ball
And laid me out limp in the mire of the kraal[211] –
And the kick retrospective, the kick, the collective
Accumulate kick one gets out of it all.
For it all totalled up to the kick that is best –
The kick that one gets from enjoying a rest.

Once my scholarship won me a kick in the pants
For proving the pyramids built by white-ants.
And still I am prone to pedantic delights.
I get such a kick from historical sights!
The kick of my heart, like a punch on the rib
To see the "Ark Royal" returning to "Gib"[212]
As that great swan of victory rippled the tide
With a hole in her decks, and a list in her side;
To see the Alcazar, reduced to mere slag,
Disdainfully waving her bullet-torn flag –
And the kick (such as maidens must dream in their beds!)
When over the Tagus we booted the Reds,
With the Crescent for Sickle, for Hammer the Cross,
And the thugs of the Kremlin behowling their loss,

---

[211] South African enclosure for cattle or sheep.
[212] Travelling from Lisbon to Gibraltar by sea on his way to join a convoy to England in July 1941 to join the war effort, Campbell saw HMS *Ark Royal*, which had been hit in action near Sardinia, limping into Gibraltar harbour.

As Herod made off with his smashed titty-bottles
To pass round the hat for the babies he throttles,
And the captured munitions were piled to such height
That it seemed that the mountains had calved overnight.

Now the kudu and sable[213] may graze on their run
For I've tried all the kicks out of life, except one.
It's a two-booted kick, to whose impact aglow,
Clean over the goal-posts of glory I go,
And never come down, but sail on, like a dove...
And it comes from the friends and the books that I love.
The best is my Muse, this companion of mine,
Who has learned, like de Lenclos, to age like good wine,
And the scent of her hair is the wind in the pine.
As black as the future that looms in our way
(I like it that colour, forbode what it may!)
Her hair is my night – but her face is my day.
With the wealth of the Muses my bookshelves are straining,
My trestles, of Bacchus,[214] as shrilly complaining.
And we say to our friends, both the living and dead,
"Be with us tonight while the table is spread."
But though with its lading my wood may be sore,
My leather is game to continue the score –
And I say to my Life "Come and kick me once more!"

---

[213] Large stout-horned black antelope.
[214] Roman god of wine and revelry.

¡Caramba![215]

Her firm proud flesh admits no queries,
Clear statement which you cannot garble,
Wherein the bust and rump of Ceres
Roll in the rhetoric of marble.
Touch but the trigger of desire
To which her beauty is the Bren[216]
With kisses she will open fire
Far worthier for gods than men.
Her tints are in the rainbow seen.
Red laughters on her lips rejoice.
Orange her hair, her eyes are green,
And ultra-violet is her voice.
I faked all that. Did she exist,
Or were she someone I had known,
I would not care. She'd not be missed.
I have one better, of my own!

Twin Reflections

Like an Atlantic roller, steep and strong,
She hit me, broke on me, and hid the sun.
I surfed a foam of roses all night long.
Day broke with two auroras. She was one.

White Pegasus,[217] with jet-blue mane astream,
Her girlhood reared and bolted me astray,
The jockey to a thunderbolt of cream
Galloping headlong up the Milky Way.

---

[215] Good gracious! (Spanish colloquial).
[216] British light machine-gun.
[217] Winged steed of Greek mythology.

Stacked thirty-high the zodiacs tiered above us
The trumpet in our blood sang out for strife.
In rushed the Minotaur.[218] It was our Love,
And both of us were fighting then for life.

When from its black toril[219] the rapture volleyed
To toss and gore us, in one shambles thrown –
To such a fall, what triumph is not squalid?
To such a death, what life is worth a groan?

Each enemy of Nature bit the ground,
Insanely bleating like a butchered beast,
For us alone the trumpets seemed to sound
Each time the throes of rapture were released.

Two scorpions curved to sting, their spines one hoop,
We seemed, that in a single death expire:
Two planes colliding as they loop the loop
Each having shot the other into fire.

Tired with our strength, the night of years grew pale,
And into waves of crimson sank the dark
To perish like an ocean-heaving whale
Torpedoed by a swordfish and a shark.

The stars, like kisses, had devoured the night
Of rage and battle, into one huge star.
And suavely into rhythm with its light
We wake at peace, and wonder what we are.

If you have seen an almond-tree in bud
Sprayed on the dawn like Biscay[220] on the piers,

---

[218] Monster, half-bull half-man, of Greek mythology; kept in the Labyrinth, and to whom Athenian youths and maidens were sacrificed until it was slain by Theseus.
[219] The toril is the door through which the bull enters the arena in a bullfight.

Flushed from within, as if with conscious blood,
Yet glittering with dew, like chandeliers –

Such is her wrestling whiteness, even yet,
Where beauty strives with age, as art with time,
But it was with her eyes, that scorn to set,
She made herself immortal and my rhyme.

In their dark fire I saw myself made younger
Star-twinned, with Castor, in the night to shine.
Far into their huge depths, with mystic hunger,
Two breathless Muses gazed at her from mine.

November Nights

On the westmost point of Europe, where it blows with might and main,
While loudly on the village-spires the weathercocks are shrieking,
And gusty showers, like kettledrums, are rattled on the pane,
The rafters like the shrouds of some old sailing-ship are creaking,
And the building reels and rumbles as it rides the wind and rain.

The treetops clash their antlers in their ultimate dishevelry:
The combers crash along the cliffs to swell the dreadful revelry,
And to the nightlong blaring of the lighthouse on the rocks
The fog-horns of the ships reply. The wolves in all their devilry,
Starved out of the sierras, have been slaughtering the flocks.

---

[220] The Bay of Biscay in the Atlantic Ocean off the coast of Spain and France, noted for its high seas.

Now peasants shun the muddy fields, and fisherfolk the shores.
It is the time the weather finds the wounds of bygone wars,
And never to a charger did I take as I have done
To cantering the rocking-chair, my Pegasus, indoors,
For my olives have been gathered and my grapes are in the tun.

Between the gusts the wolves raise up a long-drawn howl of woe:
The mastiff whines, with bristled hair, beside us cowering low,
But for the firelight on your face I would not change the sun,
Nor would I change a moment of our winter-season, no,
For our springtime with its orioles and roses long ago.

From *Fragment from "The Golden Shower"*
(To Mary Campbell)

Yet through the dust a myriad times must pass,
In gold of lilies and in green of grass,
Or in the conscious flesh that now is ours,
Our swift protean essence of delight
Until the earth has burned away in flowers –
Until the stars have eaten up the night,
And having strung, like beads upon a thread,
The changing forms in which we now appear
We in that shining revelry shall tread
Of which we act the faint rehearsals here...
For when that final rosary is told,
He who is still new-born (though none so old)
The still-unchanging Present, fold from fold
Tearing the veil, will prove to us at last
That there was never Future time nor Past,
But that, a mere illusion in each tense,
Time was the mere reflection of events,
To fill up gaps between them in our sense –

Unreal and hollow, like the footworn track
That one who travels leaves behind his back,
Or merely finds between him and his goal!
And that, instead of Time or Space, a sole
Personal *presence* occupies the whole.
When all that was, or shall be, merely *is*
And all existence is self-known in His,
That which we feel today in either sprite,
And which we know in moments of delight
Will then be fixed. If into you I burn
Or both into that All, or each return
Singly into ourselves – all shall be one.
And in our love some part of this is done,
For though He shines by us, it's not to dim
The least existence that exists in Him.

CPSIA information can be obtained
at www.ICGtesting.com
Printed in the USA
BVHW030833110722
641837BV00013B/374